WALK YOUR
BUTT OFF!

WALK YOUR BUTT OFF!

Go from Sedentary to Slim in 12 Weeks with This Breakthrough Walking Plan

SARAH LORGE BUTLER with **LESLIE BONCI, MPH, RD,**
and **MICHELE STANTEN,** former fitness director of **Prevention**.

RODALE.

The information in this book is meant to supplement, not replace, proper exercise training. All forms of exercise pose some inherent risks. The editors and publisher advise readers to take full responsibility for their safety and know their limits. Before practicing the exercises in this book, be sure that your equipment is well maintained, and do not take risks beyond your level of experience, aptitude, training, and fitness. The exercise and dietary programs in this book are not intended as a substitute for any exercise routine or dietary regimen that may have been prescribed by your doctor. As with all exercise and dietary programs, you should get your doctor's approval before beginning.

© 2013 by Sarah Lorge Butler and Leslie Bonci, MPH, RD

Photographs © 2013 by Rodale Inc.

All rights reserved. No part of this publication may be reproduced or transmitted in any form or by any means, electronic or mechanical, including photocopying, recording, or any other information storage and retrieval system, without the written permission of the publisher.

Rodale books may be purchased for business or promotional use or for special sales. For information, please write to:
Special Markets Department, Rodale Inc., 733 Third Avenue, New York, NY 10017

Prevention® is a registered trademark of Rodale Inc.
Printed in the United States of America

Rodale Inc. makes every effort to use acid-free ∞, recycled paper ♻.

Cover illustration by Alix Nicholaeff
Photographs by Tom McDonald/Rodale Inc.
Book design by Christina Gaugler
Cover design by Amy C. King

Library of Congress Cataloging-in-Publication Data is on file with the publisher.

ISBN 978–1–60961–882–7 direct hardcover
ISBN 978–1–60961–883–4 trade paperback

Distributed to the trade by Macmillan

2   4   6   8   10   9   7   5   3   1   hardcover
2   4   6   8   10   9   7   5   3   1   paperback

We inspire and enable people to improve their lives and the world around them.
For more of our books visit prevention.com.

To the test panelists,
who let me walk a mile in your shoes,
this book is for you.

CONTENTS

FOREWORD

If you've picked up this book, there's a good chance you want to lose weight.

There's also a good chance that you've tried to lose weight in the past and haven't succeeded. In both cases, I have fantastic news for you: *Walk Your Butt Off!* will change your life—and your pants size—but you must be willing to meet it halfway. If you're ready to take care of your body and put your health first, the Walk Your Butt Off! plan will arm you with everything you need to get there and ensure you have fun along the way.

How do I know? This program was created by a trio of top-notch women, all of whom have to work just as hard as the rest of us to sneak activity into our crazy-busy schedules (which is why they've created a program that doesn't require hours in the gym and can be done anytime, anywhere). They know the rewards that come from committing to daily exercise—more energy, better health, and a body that looks good in jeans and a tank top—and their enthusiasm for fitness jumps off the pages. Who are they? Well, there's your walking coach, ACE-certified fitness instructor and previous fitness director of *Prevention* magazine, Michele Stanten. There's also your food coach, Leslie Bonci, RD, the director of sports nutrition at the University of Pittsburgh Medical Center and all-around lover of real, delicious, good-for-you foods. And finally, there's writer and mom-of-two Sarah Lorge Butler, who helped Michele and Leslie put together their program in a way that's clear, concise, and enjoyable to read.

It wasn't enough for Michele, Leslie, and Sarah to create a program that should work for everyone. They wanted to be 100 percent positive that any woman who picked up this book would have success if she followed the program. So what did they do? They tested the plan on 19 real women, the majority of whom were in their 40s, 50s, and 60s. If you've already blown out your 40th birthday candles, you know that they were up against all of the challenges that make shedding pounds more difficult as you age: a slowing metabolism, hormonal changes, and a jam-packed schedule. So when these same women shed 10, 20, even 30 pounds, it became clear that the Walk Your Butt Off! program works. And it works remarkably well.

Forget dieting. You won't have to give up a single favorite food group to see results on this program. In fact, Walk Your Butt Off! doesn't even include a diet program because we know that diets don't work long term (and they only make you miserable in the short term). Instead, Leslie has shared simple, smart, totally doable tips that will help you slowly change your eating habits for the better. By incorporating these small food changes, you'll speed your results and boost your energy levels.

You will, of course, have to walk for roughly 30 minutes, 5 days a week. It won't always be easy—you'll have to break out of those sedentary chains that nearly all of us are enslaved in, thanks to desk jobs, long commutes, and the constant lure of snuggling up on the couch for some TV time. But *Walk Your Butt Off!* will inspire you to put one foot in front of the other and will give you the tools to turn a simple walk into that life-changing, magic fix you've been searching for. The rest is up to you.

My final words to you, dear friend: Look forward to your daily walks. We are required to sit so often—sometimes for hours on end—that sitting is no longer a reward. *Walking*, even for only 30 minutes a day, is a pleasure that only the truly lucky get to enjoy, and it is such a treat. Tune in to how good it feels to move your body, to breathe in and out, and, yes, to break a sweat. Be thankful you're alive, embrace the journey, and keep your sights set on the horizon. *Walk Your Butt Off!* is here to show you how.

Happy walking,
Jenna Bergen
Prevention fitness editor

INTRODUCTION

Walking gets a bum rap. A raw deal. Shafted.

The only time anyone makes a big deal about walking is when you're about 12 months old. You take your first wobbly steps toward the outstretched arms of your mom or dad before falling into the coffee table. With any luck, the other parent captures the moment on video. But after that, no one pays walking any mind.

Walking is the orphan child of exercise. It doesn't have the dramatic grunting of weight lifting, the giggling-with-your-girlfriends appeal of Zumba, the ooohm of yoga, the cutting-edge gear of cycling, or the year-round competitive opportunities that runners get. Even though walking—racewalking—is an Olympic sport (betcha didn't know that), it somehow still gets overlooked.

Because walking is such an integral part of our lives, most of us fail to notice it as a form of exercise, a vital component of good health, and a powerful tool for weight loss. From the moment we put our feet on the floor in the morning until the minute we crawl under the covers again two-thirds of a day later, we rely on our two feet to get us places—the kitchen, the bathroom, into our cars, down the hall to the copier. It's so simple, so essential to our identity as humans that we tend to not give it much thought. We think about walking only when we're in pain and can't move comfortably.

THE POWER OF WALKING

It's time to reconsider. This simple movement, for which we're designed, can work wonders.

For conditioning: With walking, you're developing the capacity of your cardiovascular system. You're also building muscle in the legs and core and, when you walk at faster speeds, the arms and shoulders.

For health and longevity: According to Dr. Steven Blair, professor of exercise science, epidemiology, and biostatistics at the University of South Carolina, a little walking can stave off many diseases. Even if you're carrying around more weight than you'd like, if you walk regularly, you're healthier than someone of the same weight who doesn't move. Walking 30 minutes a day offers protection from a host of ills, like diabetes, heart disease, and cancer. Simply put, statistics show that a little walking prolongs your life. It's better to be overweight and active than thin and sedentary. Active people—no matter what the scale says—enjoy longer and fuller lives than inactive people.

And, of course, the one everyone cares about . . .

For weight loss: Walking burns calories at a steady, reliable rate. Walk enough and you'll see results on the scale. Walk a little faster and you'll see results quicker, too. Research shows that exercise is a crucial component of maintaining weight loss. If you get the pounds off, you'll need regular exercise to help you keep them off.

What's more, walking couldn't be easier. It's low impact, requires no special gear beyond a comfortable pair of sneakers, and can be done anywhere. Even in place. An easy walk doesn't require a shower. Walking trumps all other activities in the convenience department.

For all these reasons, walking is worth a fresh look.

ASKING QUESTIONS; FINDING ANSWERS

That's what we did when we created the Walk Your Butt Off! program. We wanted to see what would happen if people walked consistently at least 5 days a week for about 3 months.

Meet Our Experts

Coach Michele Stanten has been walking, quickly, for more than 2 decades; and sometimes, when she's out doing errands with her family, she'll ask her husband to drop her a few miles from home and let her walk the rest of the way back. On a typical day working with the test panel volunteers, she was out there walking backward, her gaze trained on the test panelists, scrutinizing their form, telling this one to look up, that one to relax her shoulders, this guy to pay attention to letting his heels strike first. Michele was the fitness director of *Prevention* magazine for 20 years, and she has walked distances up to a marathon. When we entered a local 5-K (3.1 miles) road race together, she finished in 38 minutes—faster than many of the runners. When she's walking, she's *moving*.

Then we have **Leslie Bonci**, MPH, RD, CSSD, LDN, who is the director of sports nutrition at the University of Pittsburgh Medical Center. She helps everyone from individual clients struggling to lose weight to scholarship athletes at Pitt who need to eat for better performance. The most important thing to know about Leslie, though, is that she lives a normal life with a regular diet full of easy-to-find foods. It's not all kale and tofu. She shops in a regular grocery store and has raised two sons while working more than full time. And frankly, she doesn't love being in the kitchen. Instead, her husband, Fred, does most of the cooking. Leslie runs and lifts weights several times a week, and she walks daily with Fred and Chloe, their 90-pound dog.

Me, I'm **Sarah Lorge Butler**, and I'm the writer. For exercise, it's walking, running, swimming, and racing kids around the house. I always feel better during and after a workout, and call me selfish, but I'll go to great lengths to protect my exercise time. I loved working with the panelists, seeing the progress they made, and hearing about their success. Learning what they were accomplishing motivated me to get on my treadmill every morning.

Back in October 2011, we developed a 12-week walking program and recruited 22 volunteers to test it out. We wanted the test panelists to tell us—honestly—about what happened to them. Could they start an exercise program? More importantly, could they stick with it?

Did they get faster? Feel better? Gain health and energy? How did they do when the weather turned colder? When all the big-eats holidays—from Halloween through New Year's Eve—confronted them?

Of course, there was one major reason they wanted to walk: They wanted to lose weight. And, of course, we wanted to know what happened in that department, too. Could they shed pounds with walking?

OUR FEARLESS TEST PANELISTS

We had a mix of people: 19 women, 3 men. The youngest was 31; the oldest, 61. They came from a range of jobs and industries—a few information technology professionals, a school nurse, a college basketball coach, a nanny, a massage therapist. Many had young children at home. A few had grown children at home. Some had elderly parents they were caring for. Then there were seasonal challenges: the holidays, the colds and viruses they were susceptible to at that time of year, and the fact that they were exercising through short, dark, cold days.

The point is this: These people had dozens of different challenges and commitments requiring their attention. Exercise usually didn't break into their top-five priorities on an average day.

We tried to make it easy for them. So here's how we worked it: Our walking coach, ACE-certified fitness instructor Michele Stanten, gave them a weekly walking schedule, with five workouts per week. They could walk more if they wanted, but they were encouraged to try for a minimum of 5 days per week. It didn't matter if they walked Monday through Friday and took the weekend off or walked the weekend and found 3 other days to squeeze it in. They took the five workouts and did them at their convenience.

The panelists started gradually, with walks of just 20 minutes. Over the course of the 3 months, the workouts built to between 28 and 40 minutes. Twice a week, participants walked at a moderate pace of their choosing. Three times a week, we asked them to move faster, at a pace they had to concentrate on. At first, they walked at this pace for 1-minute intervals throughout a session. By the end of the program, they were sustaining that fast pace for 25 minutes at a time.

At the same time, we gave them access to Leslie Bonci, a renowned dietitian. Leslie didn't tell participants what to eat. She didn't distribute recipes or offer calorie guidelines. Instead, she focused on getting panelists to think about *how* they eat. She asked them to look at their habits and give some serious thought to where, when, why, and how much they were eating rather than focusing solely on the contents of the plate. Leslie talked with each test panelist, addressed specific questions they had, and e-mailed them once a week with an eating behavior to focus on for the next 7 days. Her eating plan started with some thought-provoking questions and then gave panelists the freedom and the tools to figure out what worked for them. They changed their eating at a rate that suited them. No one-size-fits-all diet here.

SO, WHAT HAPPENED?

We'll break down the results more closely in the following chapters. But here are the highlights:

Faster speed: Everyone walked. This we know for sure. The test panelists sent us weekly workout logs, tracking their exercise. Sure, they hit obstacles along the way, such as illnesses, a few sore shins, work travel and pressures, and in-laws who overstayed their welcome during the holidays. But we know they walked, because when the program started, each of the volunteers was tested with a 1-mile walk on a treadmill to determine their speed. Twelve weeks later, we tested them again, and every single participant was faster, whether by several seconds or several minutes. One overachiever, Sandra Hamill, cut nearly 6 minutes off her walk time!

This is great on several counts. The participants are fitter, stronger, and healthier, as the walk tests show. They're in better condition now than they were when they started. They're also getting more bang for their buck because the quicker a person walks, the more calories that person burns. And, frankly, as Dr. Blair's work points out, they're less likely to die.

Pounds shed: Of the 22 volunteers, 15 lost weight—an average of 10.4 pounds apiece. The largest amount of weight lost was 27.6 pounds in 12 weeks.

One woman finished at exactly the same weight. And although six people gained weight (modest amounts from 0.2 to 3.2 pounds), each of them reaped other health benefits from following the program. They lowered their body fat percentages, lowered their blood pressure, or shed inches. For instance, one woman who gained 0.2 pound actually dropped 4 inches from her waist.

THE RIGHT WAY TO LOSE WEIGHT

Leslie is fond of pointing out that a reasonable rate of weight loss is 0.5 pound to 1 pound per week. That's a sustainable rate—meaning, if you lose those pounds, they're not coming right back the minute you stop "dieting." We all know of a few people who dropped 40 or 50 pounds suddenly and then regained them shortly thereafter—with interest. If you read *Walk Your Butt Off!*, drop a lot of weight, and then immediately pack it back on, we'll feel we've failed you. That's not what we're aiming for. We're looking for slow, steady results. Results that last.

HAPPINESS AND HEALTH DISCOVERED

Some people will look at our results and think: *Ten pounds in 12 weeks? Might be more; might be less? That's not enough weight loss to make this program worth it.* If you're one of those, let me challenge you to redefine your scope of health and well-being.

We think that to measure the success of *Walk Your Butt Off!* solely in terms of pounds shed seems to be taking a mighty narrow view of things. Everyone is different in terms of weight and how quickly or slowly they can lose it. Some people drop pounds quickly at the beginning and plateau after that; others require 12 weeks of walking just to let their bodies know that, yep, we're doing this exercise thing regularly now. Only then do their bodies start to give up some extra weight. In fact, even though the test panel had officially ended, several of the participants with more modest weight loss, who loved the program and chose to stick with it, reported seeing more pounds disappear between Weeks 12 and 18.

More important, our test panelists reported tons of other benefits. We asked them to rate their self-image, before and after. Most improved. We asked them how they slept. Nearly all said they slept better: It took them less time to fall asleep, they awoke less frequently during the night, and in the morning, they got out of bed a little bit easier. Many panelists reported better moods, too. They were more able to handle life's stresses and had increased energy to tackle the day ahead. One participant, who has had a lifelong battle with depression, found his symptoms decreasing with regular walking.

So, sure, you can measure pounds, and weight loss is one big goal of this program for those who have some pounds to spare. But that's not the total picture. Get started at your own pace, try some walking workouts, and see how your day-to-day health picture, however you define it, is enhanced.

BE YOUR OWN COLLABORATOR

Our test panelists had the benefit of give-and-take. They e-mailed us questions; we responded. They called; we answered. Someone would mention to Coach Michele that a certain muscle was bothering her, and Michele would suggest a stretch. They confessed to Leslie about bingeing on butter cookies during the holidays, and she told them to move on and try to do better next time. They'd tell me how they missed 5 days of workouts, and I'd remind them that walking for even 10 minutes was better than nothing.

This was a collaboration. We met the test panelists where they were and helped them adapt their fitness and eating habits to become stronger. When Bill Kealey told Leslie that he liked to have one free-for-all eating day a week, she didn't flinch. She suggested that if he could reduce his intake on that day by even 200 calories or extend it to once every 10 days instead of once a week, it would make a huge difference over the course of a year.

Everyone has strengths and weaknesses in terms of eating habits. A few of our test panelists had never examined their eating habits; others had been counting calories for years. No surprise, then, that the novices—who discovered the power of fruits and vegetables, fiber, whole grains, and protein—saw more dramatic weight loss than those who had already been trying to eat a healthy diet.

The point of this panel was to help participants see where they stood and figure out what changes they were ready to make. The progress was slow but sustainable.

In the pages ahead, Michele, Leslie, and I will try to offer you all the wisdom we shared with the test panel. We hope it helps.

In the end, though, you'll have to keep your own counsel and be your own advisor. With the help of this book, you can analyze your eating patterns and see how you can work out when you thought it was impossible. But you'll still have to rely on yourself to keep going when the going gets tough. We'll pose some thought-provoking questions aimed at getting you to see the habits that help you and the patterns that sabotage your good intentions. We'll ask you to take a good, hard look at yourself. But the motivation to do this—to walk regularly and to eat in a healthier way—has to come from you. You're the coach and the athlete, the guru and the novice. Listen to yourself. Nudge yourself when you need to. Think honestly. And get ready to walk.

CHAPTER *1*

THE
First
Steps

The human body is built to move on two feet. All those millions of years ago, humans evolved as hunter-gatherers, chasing prey for long distances across the plains.

I'm pretty sure our bodies weren't destined for the hours we spend sitting still, heads bowed, captivated by Twitter. Nope, our largest muscle groups are in our legs, not our thumbs.

And that's what the experts tell us, too. Steven Blair, PED, professor of exercise science, epidemiology, and biostatistics at the University of South Carolina, has devoted his 40-year career to studying exercise and health. His studies involve thousands of people, whom he has tracked for decades. And it comes down to this: With 30 minutes of moderate exercise daily—no matter what number is staring back at you from the scale—you'll live longer than someone who sits around all day.

With 30 minutes of exercise, you'll also live better than someone who sits around all day. Dr. Blair likes this quote from Abraham Lincoln: "In the end, it's not the years in your life that count. It's the life in your years."

Moderate exercise for 30 minutes. Half an hour. That's what it takes.

We believe you can also lose a fair amount of weight by walking—and our test panel proved that to be true—but this much is clear: If you're planning to follow the Walk Your Butt Off! program, that's the minimum time you'll need—5 days a week. Sure, more is better, but you need to set aside at least those 150 minutes each week.

GET OUT YOUR CALENDAR

So, the first step in the program is finding the time. Before you take your first walk, you need to tackle this as a scheduling project.

Trust me when I tell you that the people on our test panel led really busy lives—an endless rush from job to home to kids and back again. Even their vacations were exhausting. Full days at theme parks or hours driving across parts of the country to cram in a few hours with relatives before piling back in the car again. The retirees, who sure don't act retired with their part-time jobs and classes, had commitments galore. They had to be conscious about planning their exercise or they'd get too busy to fit it in. The stay-at-home moms were frantic, and they could never be sure their tots would sit still in a stroller for 30 minutes.

Getting people to take a serious look at their schedule and find this time is, well, almost as big a lifestyle switch as asking someone to go back to school or change careers. It's a completely different mind-set to carve out time for yourself and make it sacred. Can't be done, a lot of people think.

When you're planning, you've got to figure out a time you can live with. Rodney Voisine, MD, founder of the Center for Weight Management and Wellness in Portland, Maine, counsels patients on diet and exercise during a 12-week program there. In the initial meetings, he sees a lot of people who are gung ho about exercise. "I have patients who tell me they're going to get up at 4:30 in the morning, go to the gym, come home, feed their three kids and get them off to school, and then go to work," Dr. Voisine says. "I'm like, 'Whoa, I'm already tired.' Some people might be able to do that but not a lot."

That kind of enthusiasm is admirable. But you've got to be realistic. Maybe delaying your arrival home after work so you can walk for 30 minutes is a more likely scenario for you. You might have to hire a babysitter or trade off exercise days with your spouse.

Test panelist Val Donohue, a basketball coach at a Division III college, understood that to be consistent in her exercise, she needed to take matters into her own hands. She'd leave the house in the morning wearing her walking clothes, park on the campus where she works, and start walking—all before heading to her office to turn on her computer. Even if she could squeeze in only 20 minutes on a particular day, she did not set foot in her office until she'd had her workout.

Bill Kealey, a dental hygienist who lost 11 pounds, walked $2\frac{1}{2}$ miles each way to and from work 4 days a week. It worked for him.

Whatever you choose, schedule the appointment with yourself. On a Sunday evening, plan your exercise for the upcoming week. Susan DeSmet tried that. A full-time school nurse with two teenage boys and a 5-year-old daughter, Susan would sit down with her calendar on Sunday nights and plug in the five workouts—most in the morning. Then she'd pin that schedule to her refrigerator.

I've gotten good at the Sunday Night System myself. Now it's just a mental exercise, and I don't have to put pencil to paper. You might think I'm crazy, but I schedule my workouts before just about anything else. Husband is traveling on Tuesday, so I'll get up early, check e-mails, and get the kids ready to go. Then I'll park at my daughter's school after I drop her off at 8:10 and go from there. If I'm back by 8:40, I can still shower and be at my desk for a 9 a.m. phone call.

I know how lucky I am to have a flexible schedule and a casual workplace. Still, my workouts are frequently in the morning. Clothes laid out next to the bed, alarm goes off at 5:45, I'm on the treadmill at 6, so the workout is done before the rest of the day interferes. (Here's another reason why mornings work for me: only one shower per day. I consider it a waste of time to have to shower for work and again after a workout.)

That's just me. Coach Michele, who isn't a morning person, works out midday or in the evening. She's been known to exercise at 9 p.m. or even later on some nights.

The point is this: Get out your calendar. Look at it. Where can you slot in 30 minutes five times a week? You're coming along with us on this walking program. We're thrilled to have you. But before you turn another page, get cozy with your calendar and find some time.

TIME IS OF THE ESSENCE

It's well established that everyone is strapped for time. That not-enough-hours-in-the-day sense we all carry around? We assume that's you. The Walk Your Butt Off! program was designed with busy people in mind.

If you're trying to lose weight, you need to burn calories. Walking burns 'em and burns plenty of 'em. Here's the thing, though: The faster you walk, the faster you burn calories—and the sooner you finish your workout, too.

So, the program aims to make your pace noticeably quicker. You don't have to walk so fast that you're gasping for breath. We don't want you to be so uncomfortable that you quit and go back to your sedentary ways. That's not the point. The hope is to gradually dial up the speed. Over the course of 12 weeks, your pace will evolve and will pick up to the point that a workout in the final week of the program will torch far more calories than a workout in Week 1. By the end, you'll be able to walk at a fast pace, nonstop, for 25 minutes.

How does speed help? According to the Compendium of Physical Activities, a 150-pound person walking 3 miles per hour burns about 225 calories per hour. Nudge that speed up to 4 miles per hour and that person burns 340 calories per hour.

By the end of the 12-week program, our test panelists were able to walk at a rate that was somewhere north of 4 miles per hour (4.2 on average), so if they weighed 150 pounds, they would burn 385 calories in an hour. In other words, by moving the speed up from 3.0 to 4.2, they're burning an extra 160 calories an hour. It's worth it to move fast.

At this stage, it's not important to obsess over the calories. You

┌───┐

● **Every body is different!**

The number of calories *you* burn while walking is individual. It
depends on your weight as well as your speed. The more you weigh,
the more effort it takes to walk and the more calories you expend.
A 250-pound person burns more than a 150-pound person.

└───┘

just want to get moving, with the understanding that if weight loss is
your goal, faster is better, and that's what you're aiming for by the
end of the program.

Even if weight loss isn't your goal and you're looking to improve
your health, faster is still better because walking faster will greatly
improve your cardiovascular fitness. Your heart and lungs will
become more powerful and you'll lower your blood pressure and
cholesterol.

We've got the studies to prove it. Dr. Blair's research, which followed 13,000 people over 10 years, divided those people into three
groups: low fitness (those who were the least active and at the bottom
20 percent of exercisers); moderate fitness (the next 40 percent); and
highly fit (the top 40 percent, who were the most physically active).
His results showed that a moderately fit person—no matter his or her
weight—is half as likely to die as someone in the low fitness group. If
you move into the highly fit group, death rates drop another 10 to 15
percent. In other words, just committing to a regular exercise routine
can protect your ticker and bolster your overall health.

That's why, even if the scale doesn't move the way you want it to,
you should still walk. A guy like Judd Hark gets that. He's one of the
seven test panelists whose weight nudged up slightly—0.8 pound—
after 12 weeks. But he's okay with that because, at his walk tests, he
completed a mile in 17:19 in October and then 13:20 (which is 4.5 miles

STAT SHEET

Age: 42

Total weight change:
+0.8 pound

Total inches lost:
3¼ inches,
including 1½ inches
from his waist

Walk time: Faster by
3 minutes
59 seconds

Judd Hark

Big wins: I was walking 6 days a week, even over the holidays, which was great. My family was amazed. I used to implode at night; my energy would just bottom out. Now I start walking after my daughter goes to bed, at 8:30 or 9. I'll be done by 9:30, then be up and alert and maybe do some more work for an hour or two. And no question, I'm falling asleep more easily. Exercise is critical for me whether or not I'm having a good eating day. The effect on my mood is much more important than the calories burned.

Next steps: When I have those impulse eating moments, my palliative choices are not good palliative choices. I need to really rethink what I have on hand in those times. I think that's a key component to the mindful eating, not only when you eat and why but what you are eating. That's where this program has taken me.

per hour) in January. In other words, he improved his speed by nearly 4 minutes. "You know, I was really proud of cutting those 4 minutes off," Judd says. "I feel really good about it."

As well he should. He's reduced his risk factors for all sorts of nasty health problems by walking consistently and getting his fitness to that level where he can sustain 4.5 mph for a while. The proof: He lost more than an inch from his waist and lowered his blood pressure by 32 points. By doing so, he has reduced his risk factors for heart disease, diabetes, and metabolic syndrome.

We'll get into the nuts and bolts of how he did it shortly. And we'll tell you how to do your own walk test. But first, get a handle on where you are right now.

ASSESS YOUR STATUS

Before you start walking, answer this question truthfully: How active are you? If your major exercise is pushing buttons on the remote and a big workout is standing in line at the company cafeteria, you'll need to ease into this slowly.

What we're presenting next is a program for absolute beginners. How do you know if you need it? If you haven't been doing any sort of exercise for the past 3 months, you should start here. The beginner plan will help you build your walking habit so you can stick to your exercise routine, too. Spend the next 4 weeks following the plan Coach Michele outlines below and then move on to Chapter 2.

But if you've been up and about—say, walking a dog for a mile or two every day or going to Spinning class three times per week—feel free to move on to Chapter 2. In other words, if you can walk for at least 25 minutes at a reasonably brisk pace with no problem—and stick to a routine—skip ahead to the walk test section on page 10.

And what if you fall somewhere in the middle? You've been active but not regular about your exercise? Check out the program on the opposite page, and do Weeks 3 and 4 before starting Stage 1 of the 12-week sequence, which we describe in the next chapter.

Here's Michele's easy schedule to get you up and at 'em.

4-WEEK BEGINNER WALKING PLAN

Goals:

- Walk regularly, aiming for at least 5 days a week. Walking every day is even better and will help make walking a habit more quickly.

- Build up to walking for 30 minutes most days of the week. This will prepare you to be able to do the 1-mile walk test before starting the 12-week program.

- Speed is not the focus of this plan, but you should walk at a purposeful pace, as if you have somewhere to be. (Forget window-shopping pace!) You can begin at a slower pace for 2 to 3 minutes to warm up. Slow your pace slightly for a minute or so at the end to cool down. For this portion of the program, don't worry too much about your actual miles-per-hour speed. Pay more attention to the amount of effort it takes for you to walk at a purposeful pace for 10 or more minutes during each walking workout. If you're walking on a treadmill and want a miles-per-hour pace to reference, check out the intensity chart on page 27.

A word of warning: You might look at this and think: *Ten minutes? That's nothing—I can do that anytime.* But you do want to set aside the time in your schedule. Change into comfortable walking clothes if you can. Wear supportive sneakers. Even though it's a short bout of exercise, it's still exercise, and you need to treat it as such—as a separate, dedicated part of your day that is just for you. Try to leave the poorly behaved dogs—the ones that stop to sniff every 5 feet—at home. Find someone to watch the baby. You can bring a friend or a spouse, but make sure it's someone who understands that you're not stopping.

The sooner you set aside special time for walking, the sooner walking will become a natural part of your routine—just as indispensable as *Modern Family* or brushing your teeth.

WEEKS	DURATION	SPECIAL INSTRUCTIONS
1	10 minutes	Walk for 10 minutes at a consistent pace at least 5 days a week.
2	15 minutes	Walk for 15 minutes at a consistent pace at least 5 days a week.
3	20 minutes	Walk for 20 minutes at a consistent pace for at least 3 days. On other days, you can break up your walks into 10-minute bouts done at different times during the day.
4	30 minutes	Walk for 30 minutes at a consistent pace for at least 3 days. On other days, you can break up your walks into 10- or 15-minute bouts done at different times during the day.

THE DIAGNOSTIC TEST

Now for the walk test. Assuming you've completed the 4-week introductory program or you're fit enough to start the 12-week program, you still need an accurate measure of where you are now. So how do you do that? You walk 1 mile and time yourself doing it.

This is easiest on a treadmill. Warm up for about 3 minutes at a pace no faster than 3.5 miles per hour, then stop the treadmill, restart it, and accelerate to a pace you think you can sustain for a mile. Note the time when the distance clicks to 1 mile. After the mile is over, give yourself at least 2 or 3 minutes of walking at a slower speed to allow your heart rate to drop gradually and your body to cool down.

You can adjust the speed as you go—make it faster or slower depending on how you're feeling. You want to be going at a pretty aggressive rate. Not an all-out, I'm-going-to-die-if-I-have-to-go-one-step-longer-than-a-mile pace, but a pace where you feel like you're pushing it. (You should be able to get a few words out in short sentences, but you should be breathing too hard to have an in-depth conversation.) After all, you're trying to test where you are now, and the question is this: How fast can I walk 1 mile?

If you don't have access to a treadmill, then a high school or college track would work great, especially if you can go at a time when no one else is there. Walk in Lane 1 to get an accurate measure of a mile. (If you walk four laps in the outside lanes, you're actually covering more than a mile, but Lane 1 is usually reserved for people running pretty swiftly. So, try to do it at a time of day when you won't be trampled by sprinters.) Give yourself at least 3 minutes of easy walking to warm up, then clear your watch and time yourself for the mile.

No track? Get in your car, find a flat stretch of road, and use your car's odometer to measure a mile. Or a smartphone, with any number

Stopwatch

A stopwatch is a must-have for this program to help you keep track of minutes and seconds. Yes, you can use your phone. But carrying an iPhone and looking at it while you're walking can be a little cumbersome. That's why I suggest investing in a basic sports watch.

We gave the test panelists simple Timex watches—$12 apiece on Amazon.com. Click the Mode button over to the stopwatch, press the Start button, and press Stop to stop the time. You've got your mile split. (Even my watch, the Timex T5K020, is only $30. I use all three alarms each day and the stopwatch at least five times a week for workouts—and, occasionally, to time pasta on the stove or salmon on the grill.)

If you want a slight upgrade, go for a watch with two timers. That will help you when you get to the speed-walking portion of the program.

of apps, can help you measure a mile accurately. Just remember where you start and where you end so when you do this test again in 12 weeks, you can do it the exact same way.

That's the point: Whatever way you test yourself for the mile, you want to do the identical thing in 12 weeks. Same amount of warm-up time, same place. That way, you'll be comparing apples to apples.

WHAT CAN I EXPECT?

Once you've timed yourself for a mile, write it down. We'll leave a space here:

DATE	MY 1-MILE WALK TIME	:
		(minutes) (seconds)

You can also record your preprogram mile time in the workbook at the back, where you will be able to record your postprogram mile time for easy comparison. Now, get out that calendar, count 12 weeks, and promise yourself you'll do the test again at that time. It's a powerful motivating force for working out when you know you have that check-in coming.

What can you expect? Coach Michele crunched the numbers from our test panel as well as from dozens of other walkers she has coached in the past. The numbers fall generally like this:

- If your initial mile takes you 18 minutes or longer (you're walking at 3.3 mph or slower), expect to cut at least 3 minutes off your time at the end of the program.

- If your initial mile takes you 15 to 18 minutes (between 3.3 and 4 mph), you can expect to cut between 2 minutes and 2 minutes 30 seconds off your time.

- If your initial mile takes you less than 15 minutes (faster than 4 mph), you can expect to cut between 1 minute and 1 minute 15 seconds off your time.

Knowing this, do the math to figure out what your time could be if you follow the program closely:

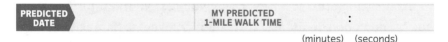

PREDICTED DATE	MY PREDICTED 1-MILE WALK TIME	:
		(minutes) (seconds)

Remember, this prediction is based on averages of walkers who have tried the program before you. You might greatly exceed these numbers, or you might not do quite as well.

Sandra Hamill was our most improved panelist. She walked 19:14 at the start of the program and sped to 13:25 by the end. That's an improvement of 5 minutes 49 seconds. Our fastest walker overall was Deb Davies, who started at 15:40 and by the end walked a mile in 12:15, a pace of nearly 4.9 mph.

Here's the crucial thing to know about Sandra and Deb: They put the work in. They followed the plan, walked at least 5 days per week, and concentrated on incorporating Michele's tips for proper walking form. And it showed in their results.

So now you've got your baseline time. You have your predicted time, a goal to hit by the end of Week 12. In the next chapter, we'll go over the workout program that will help you achieve your goal.

FOOD TALK:
GETTING STARTED

On the fall day in 2011 when we met our test panelists, we brought them over to Rodale, the corporate parent of *Prevention* magazine in Emmaus, Pennsylvania, for an orientation session. We took their pictures and recorded their data, including weight, blood pressure, and measurements at the chest, waist, hips, thighs, and arms. We asked them to rate their current self-esteem on a 1-to-10 scale. We timed them walking 1 mile on a treadmill. Then we explained the program that we were testing.

While we were going over the details of the walking program they would be starting the following week, we handed out a one-page pencil-and-paper survey about eating habits. We asked panelists to answer how many meals and snacks they ate in a typical day, if they ate differently over the weekend than they did during the week, and if they had ever "dieted." We asked them to say whether they ate slowly or quickly and if they sat for meals or ate them at a desk or in the car. Then we asked them, "If you could change one eating habit, what would it be?"

Here's a sample of their responses:

- "Reduce carbs, not emotionally eat."
- "Choose snacks that are more healthy and eat only when I'm hungry."

- "Less sugar"
- "Eliminate mindless snacking."
- "Stop binge eating."
- "Snacking at night"
- "Overeating at dinner"
- "Desire for sweets"
- "Carb intake—I love breads!"
- "Unconscious eating combined with eating too fast"

Scanning through the surveys, I could tell that most of the panelists' responses fell into three main categories:

1. Too much of something—either sugar or carbohydrates
2. Portions too large
3. Eating when they're not really hungry—what people term *mindless eating*

I loved how the one panelist wrote "unconscious eating." This made me picture a patient lying in a hospital bed, asleep, unmoving—except for his arm that reaches into a bag of potato chips and puts them in his mouth.

THE DIET ADVICE IN *WALK YOUR BUTT OFF!*

Walk Your Butt Off! is trying to help you get "mindless" out of your vocabulary. It's one thing to get into a healthy routine—such as making breakfast a bowl of Raisin Bran and half a grapefruit every morning at 7 a.m. But it's quite another to struggle with reflexive, destructive habits, like eating ice cream straight from the container in front of the TV or going for second helpings when you're already full.

Here are a few of the guiding principles behind the nutrition advice you'll find from dietitian Leslie Bonci in the following chapters.

1. **There are no quick fixes.** Sure, you could eliminate all carbohydrates from your diet for a few weeks, and you'll probably shed some pounds. However, the better move is developing habits that are sustainable for life. Weight loss diets fail because they last for a fixed time period. When the diet ends and you pick up your old habits once more, the pounds creep back on. Committing to doable long-term changes is a surefire way to lose weight and keep it off for the long haul.

2. **All-or-nothing plans are a recipe for failure.** You might resolve to give up all sugar and fat and shop exclusively at the farmers' market. Rather than attempting a sudden, radical shift in your habits—a change that will be hard to maintain—try a step-by-step approach to overhauling your eating by improving your choices one meal at a time. Prepare to bargain with yourself, compromise, and make trade-offs rather than hold yourself to an impossible set of standards.

3. **Losing weight is about more than just what you eat.** It's also about when, where, how much, why, and even with whom you eat.

4. **Solutions have to fit your life.** If you don't have time to cook, you can't be expected to follow intricate recipes. You need to develop a plan to eat well in the time you have. If that includes dinner at Subway once a week or canned soup and a tuna sandwich, there's nothing wrong with that.

Research shows it takes about 12 weeks for new behaviors to become ingrained. You can't rush this process.

You can lose weight just from walking, but if you couple exercise efforts with improved nutrition, you'll see results faster. "Anyone can exercise," says Dr. Voisine. "The ones who benefit most are the ones who also know how to eat."

This plan does not have a set diet. We're not putting out a one-size-fits-all calorie limit and sending you about your business. That might work for some people, but we're trying instead to help you see how you're eating now and how you might make a few improvements. Yes, in so doing, you'll probably change the contents of your plate, but you'll understand why you're doing that, and hopefully, you'll be making lifelong changes. We'll show you how doing so will not only help you lose weight but also help you feel great (say goodbye to mood-busting cravings and eating until you're too stuffed to move—but more on that later).

Take a few minutes now to do as our test panelists did. Before you turn the page, think about these questions: What is your biggest eating challenge? If you could change one eating habit, what would it be? Answer below or turn to page 265 in the workbook section for more room.

_____

_____

_____

_____

_____

_____

_____

_____

To-Do List

☐ Take a close look at your calendar and plan at least five times you can walk during the next week.

☐ Start the introductory walking program if you've been sedentary, or skip ahead to the **12-week program** if you've been active.

☐ Figure out how you're going to time yourself. Order a watch from Amazon.com or pick one up at Target or Walmart.

☐ Test yourself for **1 mile** and record your time.

☐ Give some thought to your biggest eating challenges.

SECRETS
of the
TEST PANEL

Age: 43

Height: 5'5"

Total pounds lost:
27.6 *pounds*
in 12 weeks

Total inches lost:
19¾ *inches*,
including 4 inches from
her waist and nearly
6 inches from her hips

Starting walk time:
16:15

Ending walk time:
13:54

Faster by:
**2 minutes
21 seconds**

Before

Kristen Tomasic

Day job: I'm a vice president of a software company that provides engineering design solutions. I'm married, with one teenage daughter.

How I got here: I was always very athletic. Growing up, I played field hockey and lacrosse. In college, I was a certified aerobics instructor. But I have struggled with my weight since college. Then, I had my daughter 15 years ago and never lost all the weight. Back in 2005, I lost 23 pounds with a high-protein, no-carb diet. But it was really extreme, and I was unable to keep it up, so I put the weight back on again. I could not get motivated the last

6 years or so. And I've always ended up with knee or back problems that put me on the bench.

How I started: I've walked before, 30 to 45 minutes at a time, but never stuck with it more than 3 months because I got bored. I would see moderate results but not enough to keep me motivated because I didn't always couple the exercise plan with good eating habits. These days, my job is really high stress, and walking alleviates that. I'm sleeping better, too. Even if I'm walking late and thinking it's going to keep me up, I hit the pillow and I'm out.

Winning strategies: I used to eat a lot of carbs. Dinner might have been 2 cups of pasta with sauce or sausage, so the big switch for me has been more protein and fewer carbs. I try to eat protein at every meal, a serving of protein the size of my palm. As far as fats go, I stick to olive oil. I'm paying close attention to the portions. Adding fiber was somewhat of a challenge. I cut out the bread, and Leslie had suggested All-Bran Bran Buds in my yogurt and on my salad to increase fiber.

I haven't totally deprived myself. I still have to live. Over the holidays, I ate Christmas cookies. Before, in one sitting, I might have eaten five chocolate chip cookies. Now I have one. And I really enjoy it, going slow and taking little bites.

Workout mind-set: I do almost every workout outside. I'm not a morning exerciser, so my walks are between 8:30 and 10 at night. I like the brisk walks, which feel like I'm going fast the entire time. I'm into my music—Rihanna and Adele. I choose fast songs so I can keep pace and walk to the beat of the music. A few times, I've found myself disappointed when I couldn't get out. I miss it when I don't go.

Extra charge: We have a bunch of hills in the neighborhood. That increases the intensity.

I'm using the Fitbit (fitbit.com). It's a tiny pedometer that tells me on a daily basis how sedentary or active I am. It graphs it out for me—shows me exactly when I was active or when I wasn't. And it can link to Lose It! (loseit.com), which is the app I use on my iPhone. I'm in the software business, so I have to use this stuff!

Follow-up: I'm at my lowest weight in about 25 years. Since the 12-week program ended, I've lost 60 pounds in 7 months and kept the weight off for the past 3 months. I will continue to walk and eat right in order to maintain my weight loss. The program has made a huge difference in my life, and I feel better than ever! It's been an amazing, inspiring, and transformative experience for me.

CHAPTER 2

Let's Move!

Over the summer of 2011, when Coach Michele and I were talking about the workouts for the Walk Your Butt Off! program, I figured I needed to learn a little something about walking.

I'm a runner and have been for the past 26 years. I also swim, bike a little, and enjoy walking with the family outdoors and exploring new trails or hikes when we're on vacation. But in all honesty, I'd never thought about trying walking as a *workout* before.

That was about to change.

One day in August, Michele and I made plans to meet at the Rodale fitness trail, which is a great path just a smidge short of a mile that loops around the fields and through the woods behind Rodale's head-quarters. I wanted her to teach me a few things about walking tech-nique and pace. But how hard could it be, really? I mean, I run several times a week, often 6 or more miles at a time. Walking, I figured, would be a piece of cake.

Let's just say I got my comeuppance. It was a really humid morning, and we were walking along at what I considered a pretty aggressive rate, although it was Michele's warm-up pace. I was starting to get a little winded while she was chattering on. I hoped she wasn't noticing how heavily her coauthor was breathing. Michele told me to swing my arms like a pendulum from the shoulder, and she had me pay attention to rolling through my feet. Heels strike first and then roll through to the toes. Those small fixes to my form helped me move more efficiently, but then Michele nudged up the speed. The sweat was dripping down my forehead and into my eyes. *Yeesh,* I found myself thinking, *when will this be over?*

We got out of the woods and onto a flat section of trail, and Michele told me to pick up the pace again—then she timed me for 30 seconds while I counted my steps. Afterward, she did a little calculation and told me we'd been walking at about 4.3 miles per hour. What? That worked out to about a 14-minute-per-mile pace. I usually run a mile in 8 minutes 30 seconds (about 7 miles per hour). Why is this so hard?

Blessedly, the workout came to an end before I embarrassed myself. We were gone for only about 20 minutes. As I caught my breath under a shady tree, Michele said a few things that have echoed in my ears ever since.

Walking is different from running; the muscles in your legs work in different ways. And walking can be a tough workout. Walkers need to recognize it as such. "I hate when people say, 'I'm only a walker,'" Michele says. "'Only a walker?' Walking is a sport in and of itself, and it's hard to walk fast. It's not just one step you take on the way to becoming a runner."

She proved her point.

Over the course of working on this book, I've developed a newfound respect for walking. And I love it, too. I'm trying to increase my pace, and right now, I can nudge the treadmill up to 4.8 miles per hour for a minute at a time before I have to ease back down to 4.5 miles per hour or so. (Michele says that she briefly hit a pace of just under 9 minutes per mile (6.7 mph) at a recent walking clinic she attended. The world's best racewalkers, like American John Nunn, who qualified for the 2012 Olympics in the 50-K racewalk, can get close to a pace of 6 minutes per mile.)

When I finish a fast walk, different muscles are sore than when I run. I feel it higher up in my hamstrings, more in my arms and back (from working on my arm swing), and in the outsides of my shins. But because it's less jarring than running, I have no pain in my joints. The aches I feel from walking are muscular aches. And those feel good because I know I'm using muscles that haven't seen any action in a while, and I feel relieved that I don't have to worry about Achilles pain, stress fractures, or calf strains—all running injuries I've had over the years.

HOW TO USE THIS BOOK

In this chapter, we're going to hit you with a lot of nitty-gritty about organizing your walking workouts. Please bear with us: This may seem like housekeeping, but it's important to start off your walking program with the right foundation. In this chapter, you'll also find Stage 1 of the Walk Your Butt Off! program.

Each stage has five workouts in it, and you're meant to complete them in a week. The following chapters will tell you what to do in each of the 11 subsequent stages.

Here's the thing, though: The workouts get a little bit harder each week. They're designed to progress gradually, so you might not notice the bumps in intensity. You could get through the program in a minimum of 12 weeks.

But if you feel like you need to stay at a certain stage for 2 or 3 weeks—or even more—that's fine, too. You can build up as slowly as you like. And if you find a week when you can't fit in at least three of your workouts or if you get sick, don't attempt to restart the program the following week at the same stage. Go back one and ease into it. If you rush through without giving each stage the attention it deserves, you'll risk injuring yourself, which would force you to take even more time off from walking.

Got it? We want you to be walking for life, and we want you to enjoy it. There's no need to rush through this and get frustrated if it's harder than you expected.

Try it and see.

THE WEEKLY WORKOUTS

The Walk Your Butt Off! program uses three different types of workouts. These workouts differ in their intensity, but they will keep you progressing toward your goal: to be able to walk faster. Remember, the faster you walk, the more calories you'll burn and the more weight you'll lose. Increasing from a pace of 3.5 miles per hour to 4 miles per hour will burn almost 100 extra calories per hour. You're going for speed.

The variety of the workouts helps keep things fresh. Our test panelists said they enjoyed trying different types of walks. Heading outside for the same 2-mile loop day after day might work for some people; others need to mix it up a bit.

Here are the types of walking workouts Coach Michele has in store for you:

- **Brisk walk:** This is a steady-paced, moderate-intensity walk. It is the perfect workout to invite a friend, family member, or coworker to join you (as long as that person doesn't hold you back).

- **Speed walk:** This walk adds short bouts of fast walking to your brisk walk. It's best to do these walks on level, paved terrain. You'll gradually add longer bouts of the fast stuff.

- **Challenge walk:** During these workouts, starting in Stage 5, you'll test yourself by walking as fast as you can for 10 or 15 minutes.

On the next page, you'll find the Stage 1 workout.

WALK YOUR BUTT OFF!

STAGE *1*

Minimum: 5 walks

2 TO 4 BRISK WALKS

After warming up by walking at an easy pace for 2 to 3 minutes, you should walk at a purposeful pace, as if you need to get to an appointment, about 3 to 4 mph, for 20 to 30 minutes. Do a minimum of 2 brisk walks this week and a maximum of 4 if you're trying to walk every day.

Total workout time: 22–33 minutes

3 SPEED WALKS

➤ Start with a 2-minute warm-up at an easy pace.
➤ Then do 4 minutes at a brisk pace and 1 minute at a fast pace 4 times.
➤ End with 3 minutes of easy walking.

Total fast walking time: 4 minutes
Total workout time: 25 minutes

INTENSITY LEVELS

You might be wondering, what do "brisk" and "fast" mean for me? Intensity levels are very subjective. As my experience with Michele on the Rodale trail revealed, her warm-up pace is my fast pace.

Your current fitness level will affect the pace you can go. Beginners will not have to walk as fast to reach an appropriate intensity level. As you become more fit, you'll find that you need to speed up to be working out at that same level. That's a good sign, showing that your cardiovascular system is becoming better conditioned.

This chart gives you guidelines for how the different paces should feel. But remember, it's highly individual.

INTENSITY	PACE	HOW	ESTIMATES	TYPE
Easy	Leisurely stroll, like you're window shopping	Light effort, rhythmic breathing; you can sing	2.0–3.2 mph	You'll use this pace at the start and end of every workout to warm up and cool down.
Moderate	Purposeful stride, like you need to get to an appointment	Some effort, breathing somewhat hard; you can talk in full sentences	3.0–4.0 mph	This pace is for your brisk walks.
Hard	Fast walk, like you're late for an appointment	Vigorous effort, breathing hard; can talk in short phrases only	3.8–5.0 mph	You'll reach this pace during the fast segments of your speed walks and on challenge walks.

A few important pieces of advice: First, listen to your body and walk at a pace that feels right to you. When in doubt, slow it down a little. And whether it's brisk walking or fast walking, pick a pace you can maintain for the entire workout. It's better to start out conservatively and increase your tempo as the workout goes on than start at a really aggressive pace that you can't possibly maintain. You don't want to start out so fast that you have to end the workout early.

Please don't drive yourself crazy worrying about these speeds. They are rough estimates, with the midpoint based on someone who is moderately fit. If you're just starting out, you'll probably hit each intensity level close to the lower end of the speed range or even below. If you've been walking regularly and are very fit, you may have to walk faster, aiming toward the higher end of the range, to achieve the recommended effort levels. If you do all your walking on a treadmill, it's easy to get caught up in what the numbers on the console say. Cover the speed with a towel, and instead pay attention to your body and do what feels right to you.

HOW TO SET UP YOUR WEEK

Here's where it's helpful to refer to your calendar. Because the speed walks are the more challenging workouts, you don't want to do them on back-to-back days. You can separate them with a brisk walk or a day off in between. But set up your week so it works for you.

Maybe it's something like this:

Monday: speed walk

Tuesday: brisk walk

Wednesday: speed walk

Thursday: off

Friday: brisk walk

Saturday: speed walk

Sunday: brisk walk

Avoid doing something like this:

Monday: brisk walk

Tuesday: speed walk

Wednesday: speed walk

Thursday: speed walk

Friday: off

Saturday: brisk walk

Sunday: brisk walk

You can rearrange the workouts to best fit your schedule. Maybe you'd rather do all your workouts on weekdays and leave your weekends completely free. But remember to keep a day of brisk walking or an off day between the speed walks.

EQUIPMENT

The beauty of walking is that you can do it anywhere and wearing anything, as long as your arms and legs can move freely. If you're comfortable walking in jeans and a hoodie, that's what you should wear. You don't have to buy any fancy clothing. Of course, technical clothing made of breathable fabrics is widely available and appropriate for walking. But you don't have to invest if you don't want to.

The three exceptions are shoes, socks, and a comfortable sports bra (for women). We'll get to shoes and socks in the next chapter.

As for the bra, you can find any variation you want with different features: hooks, crisscross backs, underwire, seamless. Try several to see what is most comfortable. You want a bra that is supportive so you're not jiggling when you walk fast. Take it for a test drive around the store. Title Nine, Moving Comfort, Champion, and Glamorise are popular brands at a range of prices, but they're just starting points.

WALKING TECHNIQUE

Is there a right way to walk? Well, as we've documented, just getting out and moving on your feet for 30 minutes at a time will help your

TECHNIQUE INDEX

TECHNIQUE #	PAGE #
1: Gaze ahead	31
2: Bend your arms	47
3: Land on your heels	72
4: Push off strong	102
5: Take short, quick steps	118
6: Swing your arms	139
7: Take advantage of gravity	156
8: Be light on your feet	170
9: Squeeze your glutes	191
10: Loosen up your hips	212
11: Swivel your hips	213
12: Pull it all together	228

Gaze ahead

Don't look down at your feet. It slows you down and can cause your back to ache. Instead, stand tall and look 10 to 20 feet in front of you. Keep your chin level to the ground, your shoulders back and down, your chest lifted, and your abs tight. This will help you increase your speed and breathe more deeply by making it easier for air to get into your lungs.

health in myriad ways. Heck, you don't even have to get out. You can march in place in front of your television if you want. Any movement, no matter what you do, is better than none.

But if you want to get faster—and we want you to get faster—then it does make sense to pay attention to your walking form. There's plenty to think about from head to toe: how your feet hit the ground, the movement of your hips, the angle you lean, the swing of your arms, even the direction of your gaze.

The photo on the opposite page shows an example of proper walking form that we will help you achieve week by week as you progress through the Walk Your Butt Off! program.

Michele will take us through a tip for improving your form during each stage. So don't try to make all the changes at once. Instead, try to master each tip during that stage. Then you'll add new ones as you continue through the program.

WRITE IT DOWN!

Once you've started walking regularly, you'll want to keep track of your workouts. Why? This is a visual, tangible way to see progress. From Day 1, if you've gone out and walked for 20 minutes (when the day before you were chained to your computer or motionless on the couch), it's a victory. Even from your first week, when the scale likely isn't moving yet, you are healthier moving than you were sedentary.

Writing it down helps you see those victories. When you have an exercise log and you do a workout, the act of recording the activity is a small reward. It also serves as motivation to keep at it. After a week, when you have more filled-in spaces than blank ones, you're psyched. And thinking about the log pushes you to go a little longer or a little more frequently the following week.

Finally, with a log, you can see how you're improving week after week, month after month. If you write down what you're doing now and keep writing it down, you'll be surprised when you look back in a month to see what you've been able to accomplish—in both speed and duration. So start the log now as a gift to your future self.

We've provided a place in the back of this book where you can track your progress, but if you prefer, there are plenty of other ways to do so. It can be as simple as a notebook with hand-drawn columns, or you can chart your workouts in a spreadsheet on your computer. Becca Kahle, one of our test panelists, became obsessed with the RunKeeper app on her iPhone.

I've got running logs that go back years. In 2012, I did a 10-K, and I was able to look back to the last time I ran that race, several years ago, and see that I had improved by 4 minutes. I was thrilled. But I enjoy filling out the logs daily. The blank spaces make me nuts.

Here's a sample workout log. We give you several pages of a blank log like this in the back of this book. Use them or log in whatever way you like—just as long as you keep track.

There are all kinds of digital solutions these days—you can join an online social community like Fitocracy (fitocracy.com) or dailymile (dailymile.com) to track your workouts or choose from a dozen smart phone apps. But personally, I'm still a fan of paper.

WALK YOUR BUTT OFF! *Workout Log*

| DATE | 4/2 | COURSE: | Jasper Park trail |

WORKOUT TIME/TYPE:

> Speed walk—25 minutes total: 2 minutes warm-up;
> 4 minutes brisk and 1 minute fast repeated 4 times;
> 3 minutes cooldown

ADDITIONAL PHYSICAL ACTIVITY

> Walked after dinner
> with dogs and husband

NOTES (INCLUDE HOW YOU FELT, WEATHER, ETC.):

> Chilly wind; felt better
> after 15 minutes of walking

FOOD TALK:

AN HONEST LOOK AT WHERE YOU ARE NOW

Can you lose weight by walking alone? Yes. If you've maintained a steady weight for years and have been sedentary, then by adding activity into your day, you'll burn more calories and eventually lose weight. It might take several weeks of walking, however, before you see results.

If the numbers on your bathroom scale have been trending upward or if you've already been exercising regularly, the surest way to lose weight is to make some changes in what you're eating at the same time as you increase your exercise.

The Walk Your Butt Off! program is here to help you work on both sides of the weight loss equation. You'll expend more calories through walking and reduce the calories you take in through eating. By making changes to both, you'll see results more quickly than if you focus on just one of the two.

As our test panelists showed, progress can be fast or very gradual. You've already met Kristen Tomasic, who lost 27.6 pounds in 12 weeks (and another 20, for 48 total, over the course of 3 months after the panel ended). Another panelist, Bethany Lee, lost no weight in the first 6 weeks, but she lost 7 pounds over the following 6 weeks. Every body is different. And every person reacts differently to increased exercise. But one trend everyone had in common was that our test panelists who focused exclusively on walking lost less weight than those who were dedicated to walking and rethinking their eating habits.

Remember the guiding principles of overhauling your food intake that we discussed last chapter: There are no quick fixes; incremental change is more sustainable than a radical overhaul; every habit should be examined—not just what you eat but where, when, why, and with whom you eat; and the changes you come up with—the solutions you find to your eating dilemmas—have to fit with your life.

THE FOOD LOG

For those reasons, we introduce the food log. This is a 3-day record of what you eat. Every bite.

Your food log will be more complete if you include a weekend day. Many people tend to eat differently on the weekends than they do during the workweek.

So, how does it work? For at least 3 days (you can log longer if you'd like), write down everything you eat. We'll show you a few samples in this chapter, and there are additional pages in the back of the book. Look for the "Walk Your Butt Off! Food Log," on page 248.

Here's an example of a food log from February 2012 that looks very familiar to me:

WALK YOUR BUTT OFF! *Food Log*

DATE 2/28

TIME:	WHAT YOU ATE:	WHAT YOU DRANK:	WHERE:
6:45 a.m.	½ grapefruit; bowl of Kashi Cinnamon Harvest with skim milk; a small amount of Wheaties Fuel cereal in milk that was left over in the bottom of the bowl	Skim milk with cereal, 2 cups coffee	Kitchen table
10:30 a.m.	Chobani Greek Yogurt, strawberry flavored	Water	Desk
Noon	Turkey sandwich on wheat with spinach, 1 slice of American cheese, honey mustard, and a pickle; 1 small Bartlett pear; 3 Thin Mints	Diet Coke	Kitchen table
3:20 p.m.	1 handful of Annie's Cheddar Bunnies; 4 carrot sticks		Standing in the kitchen
4:30 p.m.	1 Thin Mint		Standing in kitchen
5:30 p.m.	Nibble of rotisserie chicken; 4 carrot sticks	Water	Standing in kitchen
6:15 p.m.	Chicken; noodles; large serving of romaine lettuce, cucumbers, and bell peppers topped with Briannas dressing	Water and small glass of white wine	Kitchen table
8:00 p.m.	Orange sherbet		In living room in front of TV

I'D RATHER BE WALKING . . .
OR DOING MY TAXES

We realize that filling in a food log is not a fun undertaking. It's definitely a chore. It's difficult to write down everything you eat. For most of us, there are so many bites here and there between meals that logging is a project. But it's precisely because there are all those bites that it's necessary to log.

My personal food log looks pretty good and consistent up until 3 p.m. Then my kids get home, they're sitting around doing homework and having a snack, and I'm snacking with them. At 3:20 p.m., I have a handful of Cheddar Bunnies. At 4:30 p.m., one Girl Scout cookie. At 5:30 p.m., I pull a drumstick off the rotisserie chicken I bought for dinner and scarf it down while no one is watching. And that's before I sit down for dinner at 6:15.

"Mention food logs and most people shudder," says Leslie. "Why? Because you have to face what you eat. It can be embarrassing but also eye opening."

I actually saw someone shudder. On that same day we met with the test panelists for orientation, we talked about how Stage 1 of the eating plan was to keep a food log. At that point, Charlene Nelson leaned over and whispered something to the friend she came with and then looked at me with a pained expression. I asked her if that was okay, and she said, "I hate keeping a food log. I know it's good for me, but I hate it."

Join the club.

Look at the bright side, though. None of us knows what we eat unless we log it. It is not typically the meals but all the "in-betweens"—the bites of muffin, a few chips, some nuts—that mean the difference between a healthy weight and extra pounds. It all adds up, Leslie points out, but you need the log to see that.

Logging, she likes to say, brings out your inner food detective to help you troubleshoot and identify your problem eating times, foods, and quantities and what triggers those problem times.

Write It Down!

You don't have to log your food intake every day for the rest of your life. Think of this as a diagnostic test. But researchers have shown that people who keep food logs do better at losing weight and keeping it off than those who don't use them.

FOR YOUR EYES ONLY

The benefit of food logging is that it's confidential. For you alone. Unless you're working with a professional, you don't have to show your log to anyone. The test panelists, however, had to share theirs with Leslie, and some of them were reluctant to do so.

Leslie sees about a gazillion food logs a year. She doesn't pass judgment, and nothing surprises her anymore. During spring training with the Pittsburgh Pirates baseball team, she'll review hundreds of logs and make suggestions. And if you think you eat worse than a 20-year-old ballplayer, think again.

Of course, that was little comfort to some of our test panelists, who were convinced they were the worst eaters in the world. Leslie spoke with them one-on-one within the first 3 weeks of the program, and some of them were pretty hard to get in touch with. They purposefully made themselves scarce.

I got some interesting e-mails to that effect. Here's one:

```
Leslie,

    I'm so mortified at my eating habits, which is
why I haven't sent you anything. Sarah has told us
that you've seen it all, but have you seen someone
like me who has eaten a box of Devil Dogs (8 of
them) over the course of 2 days?!?! Yes, defi-
nitely mortified.
```

That was typical of the people who didn't want to share their logs. The ones who sent their logs in, well, they knew that if they were honest, Leslie could help them. By keeping an accurate food log, they were helping themselves. And they took the opportunity to have some fun. Look at this log from Gayle Hendricks:

WALK YOUR BUTT OFF! *Food Log*

DATE	Oct. 25			
TIME:	**WHAT YOU ATE:**		**WHAT YOU DRANK:**	**WHERE:**
6:15 a.m.	¾ cup Cheerios with 2% milk and 1 teaspoon sugar; whole banana		Water	Home
9:00 a.m.	6 baby carrots, 6 sugar peas, 1 ounce sharp Cheddar		Water	Job 1
12:15 p.m.	¼ (whole 8-inch) focaccia sandwich with turkey, salsa, Cheddar; 20 french fries; 2 slices dill pickle		16-ounce Dr Pepper	Job 1, cafeteria
4:30 p.m.	3 ounces pan-fried beef coated with egg and bread crumbs; leftover egg; about 4 small turnips, mashed, with 1 tablespoon butter		Water	Home (This is really too close to lunch, but I work until 10 p.m. I don't want to eat then.)
6:00 p.m.	Craving sugar. Ate more carrots and peas. Didn't help. Hershey's bar with almonds		Water	Job 2

If Gayle wasn't afraid to write what she was eating, including the Hershey's bar to satisfy her sugar cravings, you shouldn't be afraid either. In fact, by disclosing her cravings, Gayle could get help from Leslie to structure her eating earlier in the day so she could avoid cravings.

Grab a little notebook and put it in your kitchen, your pocket, or wherever it is you eat most frequently—or use the food log we provide on page 248. Call yourself and leave a voice mail to remember what you ate and when. E-mail yourself after you eat. Remember, you're your own "food detective," and your food log is the best clue you have. Don't fear it.

CHAPTER 2 ▶ To-Do List

☐ Take a look at your calendar to plan at least five times you can walk during the next week.

☐ Complete at least five workouts, including at least 2 brisk walks and 3 speed walks. Don't schedule speed walks on back-to-back days.

☐ Keep a food log for at least 3 days. Be honest. Write down every bite that goes into your mouth. You're the only one who needs to see it, so there's no reason not to be honest on your food log.

Age: 61

Height: 5'6"

Total pounds lost:
19.8 *pounds*
in 12 weeks

Total inches lost:
14 *inches,*
including 4 inches
from her hips and
3¾ inches from her waist

Starting walk time:
17:04

Ending walk time:
15:08

Faster by:
1 minute
56 seconds

Arlene Scott - - - - - - - - - - - - - - -

Before

Day job: I was a K through eighth-grade music teacher, and I retired from public school teaching in June 2007. I still substitute teach, and I give tours to school groups in Washington, DC. I'm also taking classes to help people with tax preparation. I have three grown children and three grandchildren.

How I got here: My grandmother weighed 350 pounds, and I come from a long line of people who love to eat. If I had not been a music teacher, I would have been fat. Thankfully, my job required me to move a lot, and teachers can't eat while they're teaching. I'd have a doughnut and coffee when I would leave school because I wouldn't eat all day. Then I would eat unhealthily from 3 to midnight. I've never been a binge eater overall. But in my younger days, it would not be unheard of for me to stir up a bowl of icing and eat the icing with graham crackers. I had some habits that were murderous.

How I started: I had a blood test a year ago that showed my blood sugar was high. Basically, I had prediabetes. I started walking on a treadmill—lazily—in maybe May or so of 2010. I had heard exercise was really good, so I figured I'd better get this going now before it's too late. But I didn't walk regularly until I started the test panel.

Winning strategies: Walk early in the day. I don't care if you're working, retired, whatever—if you don't get it done early, it doesn't happen.

Breakfast: I was never an eater of large breakfasts. I would drink coffee and have toast and jelly. Now I eat within the first hour of the day. That is a change for me, and I do make an effort to eat a good breakfast that I think about. I lost weight,

and I'm eating breakfast. It's kind of like, "Go figure!"

Skipping snacks: I was in a constant grazing mode. Coffee, cookies, coffee, cookies, sit at the computer. Coffee, cookies. The biggest change is that I am eating with forethought, at specific times, while I'm sitting at a table. In addition to that, I'm thinking: *What's going to satiate me? What's going to keep me calm? What's going to make me not want to reach for the cookies and the chocolate?* Christmas cookies tasted gross to me this year—and I am a dessertaholic.

Workout mind-set: I go out and start walking. I'm praying, *Wow, am I lucky to have legs and hips that still work at 61.* I warm up for at least a half mile, and 4 miles per hour is about the max for me. I enjoy walking, and I am fortunate that my body has always taken well to walking. I hiked the Rockies when I was younger and thinner. I know what it's like to do 15-mile hikes. It's like regaining that experience but with something I can actually do in my neighborhood.

Best advice: Don't wait until you're 60. When you're young and working and have kids and are pulled in 20 different directions, make time for yourself. And hang with people who give you positive messages that are healthy. It's not new: If you eat crap, it goes on your body. If you don't move, you don't burn calories. If you don't hang with positive people and do positive things, it affects your physical and mental health.

CHAPTER 3

MAKE A
Clean
Sweep

If you've turned to this page, you're at least 5 days into the Walk Your Butt Off! program. Five workouts done. Check 'em off. Put 'em in the log.

I'll tell you, and the test panelists will back me up on this, that it doesn't take long for exercise to become habitual. Sure, you might need several weeks to get used to an earlier alarm or to remember to turn the car in the direction of the gym instead of going directly home after work. But I guarantee you this: After even 1 week of exercise, if you skip a couple days that you had planned to work out, you'll miss it. You'll feel vaguely uncomfortable and start to get the nagging sense that the day hasn't been quite right. Incomplete somehow.

Coach Michele's program builds in 2 off days each week, knowing perfectly well that we can't all be Cal Ripkens. Life gets in the way. But if you have time to walk every day, by all means do so. Even a 10-minute stroll on a day you don't have a formal WYBO! workout scheduled is worth it. Know that every little bit of extra movement helps get you into shape. If you tally up your minutes of walking at the end of each week, hopefully you'll see that sum growing week in and week out.

To the right is the Stage 2 workout and a few pages later, the Stage 3 workout. The total minimum time for Stage 2 is the same as last week: 1 hour 59 minutes. If you can add 5 or 10 minutes, that's progress. And even if you can't this week, the fast walking increases slightly so you're doing more than last week.

WALK YOUR BUTT OFF!

STAGE 2

Minimum: 5 walks

2 TO 4 BRISK WALKS

After warming up by walking at an easy pace for 2 to 3 minutes, you should walk at a purposeful pace, as if you need to get to an appointment, about 3 to 4 mph, for 20 to 30 minutes. Do a minimum of 2 brisk walks this week; a maximum of 4 if you're trying to walk every day.

Total workout time: 22–33 minutes

3 SPEED WALKS

➤ Start with a 2-minute warm-up at an easy pace.

➤ Then do 3 minutes at a brisk pace and 1 minute at a fast pace 5 times.

➤ End with 3 minutes of easy walking.

Total fast walking time: 5 minutes
Total workout time: 25 minutes

A LITTLE PATIENCE

With this workout, the interval between the fast walking segments is shorter by a minute. Instead of 4 minutes of brisk walking between the fast minutes, you're down to 3 minutes. As a result, you keep the total workout time to 25 minutes but add an extra minute of fast walking.

It's a subtle change. You might be tempted to blow through this stage and the next few and get on to something more strenuous. I say don't rush it. Be nice to your body. You're asking it to move in ways it probably hasn't in quite some time, so give each stage the attention it deserves.

The Stage 3 workout, which you'll come to in a few pages, is very similar to Stage 2; the rest interval between the fast segments continues to shrink. Give this workout the full week it needs. The gradual transition will work in your favor; hurry it and you risk frustration or falling off the wagon. "What seemed to work for me was how slowly the program started," Susan DeSmet told us. "It built up over time. That really made a difference instead of having to go out there and conquer the world." If you feel like you're not getting enough work in, add time to your brisk walks or add extra brisk walks each week.

Also, when you make the shift every fourth minute from brisk walking to fast walking, there should be a noticeable difference in the pace. Refer back to the intensity chart in Chapter 2. You should be breathing a little harder and stepping at a faster rate. We'll get more into the technique of speed shortly. But by the end of that minute, when you back off into your brisk pace again, you should feel the downshift in pace. If the fast segments are too easy—walk faster!

You may not think so, but the movement of your arms helps increase your speed. So, pay attention to this stage's Technique Tip, which might just be the single most important adjustment you can make to walk faster.

Bend your arms

You wouldn't run with your arms straight at your sides, because it would slow you down. Same goes for walking. Like a pendulum, the shorter your arm is, the faster it swings. And because our bodies like to be in sync, your legs will speed up to stay coordinated with your arms. Bend your elbows 90 degrees and swing your arms forward and back. (Avoid side-to-side motion.) Keep your hands in relaxed fists and your shoulders down, not scrunched up toward your ears.

Keeping the 90-degree angle, work on pulling your elbows back behind you, so your hands swing back slightly behind your hips. It might seem counterintuitive, but this backward swing of the arm will help propel you forward faster.

DON'T BELIEVE US? TAKE IT FROM AN OLYMPIAN

Remember our racewalker, John Nunn, from page 23? He made the US Olympic team as a racewalker in 2004 and 2012. I asked him how I could get faster walking, without having to devote hours to learning racewalking techniques. Here's what he told me:

"Something that people ignore is the arms. They don't realize the role the arms play in propelling you forward. If you see people out and they're trying to work hard with their lower extremities, they can be a lot more efficient and move at a quicker rate if they include their arms in the sequence. If you're pumping everything out in front, that's good for running. With walking, bring your arms only to about midchest but pump them backward. That will help propel you forward."

Here's one more great thing about the arm motion when you're walking fast: It directly counteracts the hunched-over posture most of us assume when we're working at a computer, driving, or gazing at our smartphones. You know the posture I'm talking about—shoulders forward, neck bent, chin down. I'm pretty sure that in a few years, evolutionary charts will show human beings going from all fours to upright to the fetal position clutching a mobile device.

That position doesn't do much for our appearance. But walking is an antidote. Work on driving your arms back, and it will do wonders for your posture—Mom will be so proud! As you gain strength and tone in your back and shoulders, you'll be able to sit straighter at your desk and in your car. You'll be able to breathe easier. And you'll have fewer of those cricks in your back and neck that send you running for the Advil or contorting yourself as you try to ease them. According to a 2011 study from the University of Florence, a structured program of strength, flexibility, and posture exercises offered patients relief from back pain. Here's to that.

As promised, here's the Stage 3 workout:

WALK YOUR BUTT OFF!

STAGE 3

Minimum: 5 walks

2 TO 4 BRISK WALKS

After warming up by walking at an easy pace for 2 to 3 minutes, you should walk at a purposeful pace, as if you need to get to an appointment, about 3 to 4 mph, for 20 to 30 minutes. Do a minimum of 2 brisk walks this week; a maximum of 4 if you're trying to walk every day.

Total workout time: 22–33 minutes

3 SPEED WALKS

➤ Start with a 2-minute warm-up at an easy pace.
➤ Then do 2 minutes at a brisk pace and 1 minute at a fast pace 7 times.
➤ End with 3 minutes of easy walking.

Total fast walking time: 7 minutes
Total workout time: 26 minutes

IMPROVE YOUR FLEXIBILITY

As you start walking regularly—and at a faster pace—don't be surprised if you start to feel a few aches and pains in your legs. It's perfectly normal to have a little muscle soreness as your legs get used to the new routine. If you're walking for 2 hours or more each week, and you hadn't been doing any exercise before, there's bound to be a period of adjustment. The most common areas where you'd feel tightness are in the hamstrings, hips, quads, and shins—especially those muscles in the front of your legs on the outside of the tibia, or shinbone.

The greater your flexibility, the easier it will be for you to increase your speed as the program goes on. One of the test panelists, Denise Getchell, is a licensed massage therapist, and she told me that she knows right away which of her clients stretch. The ones who don't, she says, "have a lack of flexibility in their muscle tissue, restricted range of motion, and usually the massage causes more discomfort in a client who doesn't stretch."

Try to stretch after a walk, when you're fully warmed up. If you haven't been moving and you try to stretch, you risk pulling something. (This is supposed to help, not hurt!) Sure, stretching is one of those chores that we'd all probably rather skip. But it's important to do it so you can keep walking. Coach Michele offers some stretches to help alleviate any discomfort you might feel and, just as important, improve your flexibility and range of motion.

Full Body Forward Bend

Place your hands on a hip- to waist-high railing, counter, or table. Walk your feet back until your body forms a right angle with your head between your arms, your back flat, and your feet below your hips. Slowly lean away from the railing to feel a stretch through your arms, shoulders, and back. Lift your glutes (butt muscles!) and tailbone toward the ceiling to feel a stretch down the backs of your legs. Hold for 10 seconds. Repeat three times.

Quad Stretch

Stand tall and position yourself within arm's length of a stationary object, such as a wall or a pole, for balance. Using your right arm to keep balance if necessary, reach back with your left hand and grasp your left ankle behind you so you bring your heel up near your buttocks. Bring your tailbone forward, flattening your lower back, to feel more of a stretch in the front of your thigh. Hold for 10 seconds, then repeat on the opposite side. Do this three times with each leg.

Hip/Glute Stretches

Standing: Stand with your right side facing a wall and place the palm of your right hand against it. Cross your left leg over your right leg and lean to the left, pressing your right hip out to the side to feel a stretch. Hold for 10 seconds. Turn around to stretch the left side. Do this three times with each leg.

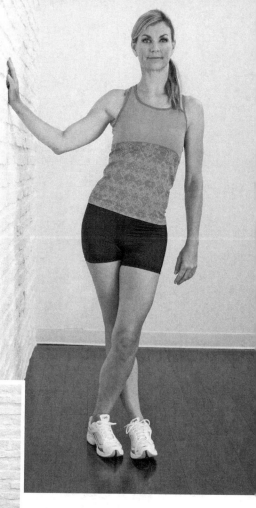

Seated: Sit on a sturdy chair. Place your left ankle over your right thigh. Sit tall, then press gently down on your left knee and lean forward slightly, feeling a stretch in your left buttock. Hold for 10 seconds. Do this three times with each leg.

Shin Stretch

This move is best done barefoot. If needed, stand near a wall or a railing to hold onto for balance. Stand with your right leg crossed in front of your left. Point the toes of your right foot so the tops of your toes are on the floor. Bend your left knee slightly so it gently presses into your right leg. You should feel a stretch in your right shin and the top of your right foot. Hold this stretch for 10 seconds. Do this three times with each leg.

Alternative: You can stretch your shins even when you're sitting at a desk working. Cross your right leg over your left and draw circles in the air with your toes. Move your feet in clockwise and counterclockwise directions. Stretch both sides.

FOOD TALK:

LOOK AT YOUR LOG

By now, you've finished at least 3 days of keeping a food log. It's time for some detective work. Ask yourself, "What did I learn?"

Read your log and try to look at it objectively. Did anything jump out at you about your eating? Is there one part of your day or week that needs improvement? Hopefully, this period of logging has helped you realize something about your food patterns that you weren't aware of before. This is part of the "train the brain" approach to eating, which will help you develop a personalized eating strategy that's going to work for you to be healthier in the future.

And here's one more question while we're at it: Back in Chapter 1, we asked you what you think your biggest eating challenge is and what one dietary habit you'd change. Now that you're keeping a food log and you have an official record of what you're consuming, are your answers to those questions still the same? Is the biggest eating challenge you listed 2 weeks ago still the biggest eating challenge or do you think it's something else?

☐ Yes. After completing a food log, my instincts are confirmed. My biggest eating challenge remains what I listed in Chapter 1.

☐ No. After completing a food log, I can see what needs to change. My biggest eating challenge is actually _____

_____

_____

_____

_____.

Leslie's patients sometimes get frustrated when she asks them to do this. They'll ask her, "Why don't YOU tell ME what to do?" She responds by saying: "I'm not you. I can't tell you what to do." The change and the recognition have to come from you. This exercise requires you to self-reflect and draw some conclusions, but it will be worthwhile. In the end, when you do change your habits, you'll know why you're doing it and you'll be able to sustain the change. One-size-fits-all diets just don't work; you need to personalize the plan to your particular challenges.

Here's another revealing e-mail we received soon after the food logs were complete:

Sarah/Leslie:

   Well, if I had any doubts about why I'm overweight, I don't now. Ugh . . . I never really took the time to stop and record what exactly I'm putting in my body. It's not a pretty sight. I think I've identified the "why" for myself, as far as why I eat the way I do: extremely busy work schedule & picky-ness. I am SO picky . . . and that's the main reason I don't know what to do to "fix" this food situation. I know myself well enough to know that I'll never be successful with a diet change if it forces me to consistently eat foods I don't like. Help!

Give her credit for saying it like it is. Despite her anguish at her eating habits, it was satisfying for her—and for Leslie—to see the light-bulb go on in her head. Leslie suggested different foods this participant could try and different preparations of the foods she knew she liked. Leslie also recommended some swaps. Fruit in place of breadsticks, and so on. It helped.

You've gone to the trouble of keeping a log. It would be a mistake to shove it in a drawer somewhere or store it in a file on your computer and never bother to look at it. It's not keeping the log that is going to help you—it's reading and understanding what's in it that is the key to success.

I know I eat really well through lunch, and then my day takes a turn for the worse with mindless snacking when my kids come home from school and I'm cooking dinner. I can see from my food log that an hour

Win the Battle at the Store

Many people who have slimmed down and kept the weight off say it's easier to win the battle at the grocery story. Even though most grocery stores are set up to overwhelm your senses with bakery items right at the entrance, if you can pass them by (and pass the snack and ice cream aisles, too), you'll be okay.

Americans don't typically shop with resolve. According to a 2012 study by Point of Purchase Advertising International, 76 percent of grocery choices are made in the store, and 55 percent of purchases are unplanned. Only 24 percent of purchases are planned.

You want your percentage of "planned purchases" to be higher. Write a shopping list and stick to it. Give yourself a pep talk before entering the store. Hold yourself to a budget to avoid impulse buys (which are dangerous because impulse buys usually consist of pies and chips, not grapes and kale). Coach Michele's family has an electronic list, which they print and hang on the fridge. Each week, they circle the items they need. Foods such as ice cream and chips are not on the list. If the Stantens decide they want to buy a "splurge" item, they have to handwrite that food on the list, and they're not likely to write more than one or two (if any) each week. They've been using this strategy successfully for more than 10 years.

You *can* win the fight at the store. The much harder battle is holding back from eating those high-calorie, high-fat items once you have them in the house.

or two after dinner, I start to nibble on the sweets a little more than I need to. (Do I really need to dip my hand in the box of Wheaties Fuel cereal at 9 p.m.? It's not healthy, not to mention kind of gross. Why do I even buy that sugary stuff?)

With Leslie's help, I've realized that if I have a more substantial lunch with a little extra protein, I'm not so hungry in the late afternoon. As for the nighttime munchies? I'm trying to savor my small dish of sherbet, then brush my teeth and call it a day. It's a work in progress, but it's an effort based on reality, not guesswork.

LAYING THE GROUNDWORK

Before you even start overhauling your diet, a little more preparation can be helpful. You want to skew the odds of success in your favor. Logging your food intake is part of that. So is thinking about your eating environment and how you can set yourself up for success.

CANDY, SWEETS, CHIPS, OH MY!

Our test panelists started walking at the end of October 2011. Right before Halloween. Their houses were stocked with candy for trick-or-treaters.

Then we had a freak snowstorm on October 29. Most of our panelists live in the Lehigh Valley, in eastern Pennsylvania, where trees fell and power was knocked out for days. It was a mess.

So here we are, 6 days into a test panel, we get a snowstorm, and in the aftermath, it's impossible for anyone to cook. Food rots in the fridge, and Halloween is canceled in most towns. What is there to eat? Halloween candy!

It was really, really difficult to eat well during that period.

And exercising was impossible, too—first because the roads were unexpectedly slippery and slushy, and then because spending the

Denise Getchell

Age: 46

Total weight change:
+0.2 pounds

Total inches lost:
6½ inches,
including 1 inch from
her waist and 2 inches
from her hips

Walk time: Faster by
1 minute
44 seconds

Big wins: What worked for me was being honest in filling out that food log. That helped me be realistic about what I was eating. It's the only way you can make changes. Also, I started making sure I wasn't distracted when I ate. I live with my boyfriend—who can eat an entire bag of chips and not gain weight—but together, we worked on creating a sacred space for eating, which is something I learned at yoga. When I stopped eating in front of the TV, I started to chew my food. Before, I would swallow my food before I had even chewed it. Now I take time to enjoy it, which helps me stop eating before I get too full.

Next steps: Unfortunately, I was really sick with repeated sinus infections during the program. I got through the first 5 weeks walking five times each week, but then I missed a lot of workouts. When we were doing final measurements for the test panel, I was just getting back to walking regularly. I was pleased I could do the mile in 16:39 at the end. It was great to have a goal with walking. I never had a goal before, except to get out and move, and then I'd get distracted and go too slowly. Now I want to complete the program in its entirety to see how I do.

day shivering in a cold house seemed to sap all energy for walking.

After a few days, the snow melted, and when the lights and heat finally came back on, we were all able to get back on track. And several test panelists decided to chuck what was left of the Halloween rations.

Sometimes, you just have to do it. Get it out of the house. Clean out anything that's going to sabotage your efforts at being healthy. Those half-eaten bags of chips, pints of premium ice cream, and towering sleeves of chocolate chip cookies? They need to go to neighbors or friends—or just into the garbage.

This lesson came suddenly to the test panel, but it helped them because the Halloween-That-Wasn't of 2011 was just the beginning of the eating season. Then we had Thanksgiving, Christmas, and New Year's. After that, we had a few weeks off, but Super Bowl Sunday has become a pretty big American pig-out, too. In fact, there's an excuse for overindulging just about any time of year. When I wrote *Run Your Butt Off!*, those panelists started exercising right before Easter. And many people logging their food intake owned up to the volume of Cadbury eggs they were eating *just because they were there.*

Think about your eating environment. Are there changes you need to make to your surroundings before you even start an exercise and diet program? "If you're going to try to be successful, get the most out of the walking program, and make the changes to your body that you want to make, you don't really need all those detractors around," Leslie says. "Sweets and junk food will just slow you down."

WHAT ARE YOU GOING TO EAT?

Now that you've gotten rid of the junk food, what will you eat instead? What do you like? When you have a craving for something sweet or salty, do you have a healthier substitute on hand that will satisfy you? Think in advance about what you're going to eat when you're hungry.

Just as you've (hopefully) gotten into the habit of scheduling your workouts, try to apply a little planning to your eating. Take a look at your week, anticipate some of your busy times, and decide how you'll handle them.

Are you traveling a lot for work this week?

Do you have meetings that go late?

Are you shuttling the kids to different activities, leaving you short on time to prepare dinner?

Do you have extra time on weekends when you could prepare a few dinners ahead of time and freeze them?

Are you prone to evening munchies, and do you need something to satisfy you without going overboard?

ADDITION AND SUBTRACTION

If you don't know your problem times already, your food log should help you figure this out. The point is that if you're preparing your eating environment for a healthy overhaul, it's not just a matter of subtraction (throwing out the junk food). It's also about addition—having healthy alternatives on hand.

Here is a little back-and-forth I had about this with Leslie:

We have nights when the kids have practices that end late or someone has a late meeting. Basically, everyone comes in late and we're all starving. What do we do?

Leslie: *Eggs. Scrambled eggs on whole grain toast with salsa on top or a little salad on the side. Or soup. Buy some sort of chunky vegetable soup—any brand you like. Dump in a pouch of microwavable rice, a can of beans or a can of chicken breast, and maybe some frozen vegetables, and everyone is eating within 10 minutes. You're not cooking, but you're eating something that seems hearty and will fill everyone up.*

Of course, just having the eggs and soup on hand takes a trip to the supermarket and some planning to have the ingredients you want. When you're putting together your workout schedule, try to plan the menu, too. When will you be at home, what will you eat, what ingredients do you need to buy? When will you be eating out, and if so, where are you going?

Q I know you're saying to throw out the Häagen-Dazs this week. But I really, really, really crave something sweet in the evening.

Leslie: *How about a Skinny Cow cone, which is 150 calories? Would that do it? Be honest with me: Are you going to eat all four cones that come in the box in one sitting? I've had clients who will do that. If you are, then you can't have those in the house either. But you can stop on your way home and buy one single-serving item like that to eat at night.*

Q I'm sitting in my office, and the cupcake in the cafeteria has my name on it. What can I eat that gets me through the "witching" hour and that tastes good and gives me energy for the afternoon work?

Leslie: *The best plan of action is to have something with you. That said, I am not a fan of a desk stuffed with anything as you may find yourself eating your way through your desk drawer. So bring one item per day: a bar such as Luna, NuGo, Kashi, or FiberPlus; two lite Laughing Cow cheese wedges with a serving of Special K crackers; or a Vita Tops muffin, which is creamy, similar to a cupcake, but lower in calories with more protein and fiber. Also, make sure you have a glass of water with lemon for flavor or a mug of tea to help you feel fuller.*

Q I am so tired of cooking every night, but I am really afraid that if I eat out or do takeout, I will overindulge. What can I pick?

Leslie: *If you eat out at a restaurant, focus on the protein—and make sure it's grilled, broiled, or blackened. Cajun-style is always a good choice. You can ask for double vegetables instead of the rice, pasta, or potato. When the family decides on Chinese, how about a shrimp or veggie stir-fry over a little bit of rice? Or if you want Mexican, fajitas are a great choice. Load up on the lettuce and salsa, chicken or steak, and the beans, and be stingy with the cheese, sour cream, and guacamole. Or just get the meat, veggies, and maybe half of the tortilla if it is enormous, and add your own Greek yogurt at home to give you more protein but less fat and calories.*

To-Do List

☐ Take a look at your calendar to plan at least five times you can walk during each of the next two weeks.

☐ Complete at least five workouts, including at least 2 brisk walks and 3 speed walks. Don't schedule speed walks on back-to-back days.

☐ Try building time in your schedule after your walks for some light stretching. It doesn't need to take more than 5 minutes to go through the moves described in this chapter.

☐ Look at your food log. Is there anything on it that surprises you? What one habit would you like to change for the better or during what time of day would you most like to improve your eating?

☐ Look at your schedule to write up a rough plan of your meals. On evenings when you're home late, what will you have for a healthy dinner?

☐ Toss the junk food that's holding you back. If you want to be successful with exercise and weight loss, it helps to have an environment that promotes success. Get rid of the detractors. Plan alternative healthy snacks to replace what you're throwing out.

SECRETS
of the
TEST
PANEL

Age: 46

Height: 5'4"

Total pounds lost:
12.4 pounds
in 12 weeks

Total inches lost:
11 inches,
**including 3¾ inches
from her waist and
2½ inches from her hips**

Starting walk time:
15:57

Ending walk time:
12:41

Faster by:
*3 minutes
16 seconds*

Before

Susan DeSmet - - - - - - - - - - -

MAKE A CLEAN SWEEP

Day job: I'm a school nurse in an elementary school, married, and a mom to three kids, ages 16, 14, and 5.

How I got here: I've been heavy since I was in the third grade. I was active as a teen, though, playing basketball and skiing. After college, I would go through periods when I wouldn't be doing any exercise. And then I'd get disgusted and I'd start doing something again. But I was off and on for most of my adult life. By the time I started with Walk Your Butt Off! I really wasn't moving well.

How I started: When I started with the program, I had reached a point where I didn't feel like I was making any progress. I would do a Spinning class or a Pilates class a few times a week. Then, the gym I was going to closed. I had never really thought about walking before, but it has turned into "my thing." Now I feel like I gotta get out there and walk.

Winning strategies: If there's one change I've made in my diet, it's that my quantities are less. I don't eat until I'm full, full, full. I'll stop at a normal-size portion, wait a little bit, and it registers. I'll tell myself, "I'm good. I'm satisfied." I'll have a little bit of whatever the family is eating and fill the rest of my plate with extra vegetables, like spaghetti squash or broccoli rabe.

Workout mind-set: I'm rarin' to go. On workdays, I go at 5:45 a.m., a little later on weekends. I'm about 60/40 outside and on the treadmill.

I always found the challenge walk really hard. I would look at the schedule and go, "Okay, that's only 15 minutes, but it has to be as fast as you can go." Then you get all the way out someplace, and you have to get all the way back.

I think my favorite was the brisk walk. I was keeping a decent pace, but I didn't have to really push it. With the speed walks, I found myself building up to a pace that I felt, *Wow, this is really good.* I jotted some notes along the way, and when I looked at my notes from October, I noticed how slow I was walking. I compared that to my notes from the end, and I'm walking so much faster.

When I first looked at the pace guidelines and the top speed was at 5 mph, I was thinking, *Omigod, who could walk at 5?* Now I'm doing intervals at 5. Just 3 minutes at a time, but I'm hitting it.

Best advice: I think sometimes people look for "the answer" about what to eat. There is no one answer. People need the tools, and then they have to work them into their lifestyle.

What seemed to work for me was how slowly the program started. It built up over time. That really made a difference.

Take a deep breath: When I get home from work, I go up to my bedroom, change my clothes, and sit down with my legs up on a chair for a few minutes, lights out. It's a time to wind down and take a break from my first job before I start my second job taking care of the kids. I think that time out of the kitchen and away from the hustle and bustle keeps me from reaching for the cookies to calm myself.

CHAPTER 4

PUT Some Muscle Into It

Everyone likes walking. What's not to like? Have you ever heard anyone who has healthy joints say they don't enjoy walking?

After all, from an evolutionary perspective, we're designed to walk. I'm not so sure we're designed for swinging kettlebells around the gym or for lying on a Pilates reformer. To get to a Spinning class, you really have to plan your day. But you can take a walk anytime, anywhere, wearing anything.

That simplicity is also one of walking's greatest drawbacks. Because we know we can walk at any time, we put it off and put it off until the day is shot. Spinning? You know you need to be there for class at 5 p.m., water bottle full. But when it comes to walking, if you don't set your mind to it, the workout can slip through the cracks.

LOCATION, LOCATION, LOCATION

One thing that's going to increase your chances of success is ensuring that you don't have to commute to your workout.

This is what we discovered from the people testing out the Walk Your Butt Off! plan: When they could click on their stopwatches at the end of their driveway, when they could walk straight from the office, or when they had easy access to a treadmill—either in their own home or at work—they were much more likely to complete their exercise routine.

It makes sense. Who wants to get in the car to keep fit? It only adds an extra layer of inconvenience, requires more time, and erects one more barrier between you and what you actually want to be *doing*. Those 10 minutes of travel time between home and gym or park can mean the difference between walking and not.

What's great about walking, though, is you really can do it anywhere. A few days after our freak October snowstorm, Coach Michele met with members of the test panel to help them out with their walking form. There were still snowdrifts along the sides of the road where the plows had come through, so she chose a parking lot for us to practice in. The lot couldn't have been more than 50 yards from end to end. But it was flat, clear of all ice and snow, and empty.

She had us walking back and forth, in long ovals, so she could see our steps. But for members of the test panel, the location of the workout was just as important a lesson as Michele's tips were. Walking can happen in the most mundane locations. Becca Kahle, who has two young boys at home, fretted about missing her workouts when her husband was traveling for work. After that day in the parking lot, she started walking at 6 a.m. in her long driveway on the mornings she was the only parent at home. Her boys knew that if they woke up early and needed her for something, they could just call to her out the front door and she'd come in.

She might have been stuck on her property, but the idea was liberating: A step is a step, and a walk is a walk. Knowing you can work out through an airport, along the halls of a hotel, or on your driveway opens up all sorts of possibilities. No more excuses about not being able to hit the gym.

You can even walk in place in front of the TV. No, you can't get the same form going when you're walking in place as you do when you're covering some ground. But you're standing and burning calories instead of being parked in a chair. It's worth trying during commercial breaks—not to replace your regular workout but to augment it.

Wherever you choose to walk for the Stage 4 workout, realize that this week is a turning point. You're alternating brisk to fast walking for even intervals, 1 minute apiece. Take a moment to appreciate how far you've come already—from 4 minutes of fast walking to 10 minutes of fast walking in a few short weeks.

If you've been walking outside, you'll probably notice that you're covering more ground in your speed walks. After all, with this workout, you're spending more than double the time walking at a fast pace than you were in Stage 1, and that will be visible to you by looking at your surroundings. You'll get a few more houses or telephone poles up the road or you'll cover more of that trail at the park. You might need an extra lap around the athletic fields. It's the same on the treadmill if you're checking your mileage at the end of the workout. Your 25 minutes this week will get you farther than the 25 minutes in Stage 1. Keep a note of this victory in your exercise log and find encouragement in it. It should make you feel good—this is progress!

Coach Michele's Technique Tip in this stage will also help carry you farther (you'll find it on page 72).

This heel-to-toe motion comes naturally to some. You might already be doing it without having realized it. For others, it's hard to get away from the heavy clomp-clomp-clomp of your entire foot striking at once, and this tip will require a little concentration to get the proper motion integrated into your stride.

Rolling from heel to toe also helps build up the shin muscles—the anterior tibialis—on the front of your lower leg. If you start to feel discomfort in that area, give particular attention to the shin stretches we went over in Chapter 3.

WALK YOUR BUTT OFF!

STAGE 4

Minimum: 5 walks
Strength workouts*: 2–3 times

2 TO 4 BRISK WALKS

After warming up by walking at an easy pace for 2 to 3 minutes, you should walk at a purposeful pace, as if you need to get to an appointment, about 3 to 4 mph, for 20 to 30 minutes. Do a minimum of 2 brisk walks this week; a maximum of 4 if you're trying to walk every day.

Total workout time: 22–33 minutes

3 SPEED WALKS

➤ Start with a 2-minute warm-up at an easy pace.

➤ Then do 1 minute at a brisk pace and 1 minute at a fast pace 10 times.

➤ End with 3 minutes of easy walking.

Total fast walking time: 10 minutes

Total workout time: 25 minutes

For the strength workout, see page 75.

• Land on your heels

As your leg swings forward, your heel should be the first part of your foot to hit the pavement. Focus on keeping your toes up as you land.

Then roll from your heel to your toes as smoothly as possible. Finally, push off with your toes to propel you forward. (Read more about pushing off in Technique Tip #4 on page 102.)

THE RIGHT SHOES FOR WALKING

As you begin to pay attention to how your foot hits the ground, you'll also want to give a little thought to the shoes you're using for walking.

Any supportive sneakers will do for your first week, especially if you're starting with the introductory program. Running shoes or cross-trainers will work fine. Even now, when we're at about 2 hours of total walking time, you might find your sneakers still have some life in them. I'm naturally suspicious of any exercise program that tells you the first thing you have to do is go drop $100 or more.

But as your speed and distance increase, and especially if you're feeling any kind of aches and pains, you'll need a new pair. Do yourself  a favor and head to a specialty running store. While large sporting goods stores and outlets have less expensive offerings, unless you get lucky, you won't find sales clerks who are trained to specifically help walkers. You don't want the guy who knows golf equipment to be helping you select new kicks.

Get yourself to a specialty running store and tell a person working there what you're up to: You're doing a walking program and need shoes that are good for walking. You'll want a decent amount of support, especially if you have pounds to shed. But you're also building up your speed, and your shoes need enough flexibility at the ball of the foot to allow your foot to roll from heel to toe and to push off strongly.

If they're good, the folks at the store will watch you walk and give you a variety of makes and models to try. And you can usually try them out around the block or on an in-store treadmill. Take them for a test drive, long enough to see how they feel. Don't feel pressured to make a decision. No one should be rushing you.

HEEL HEIGHT

For walkers who are concentrating on speed more than weight loss, beware the inches of added cushioning in the heels of many running shoes. That extra padding can make it harder to strike heel first. You do want some support and cushioning, just not so much that it's difficult to walk properly. Says Olympian John Nunn: "Because we're landing on our heel, we need something lower. Otherwise, that's more energy expended to get the foot up to land on your heel if the heel of the shoe is bigger."

BEND YOUR SHOES

Sneakers vary widely in the amount of flexibility they offer at the soles. Some shoes are like steel. The bottoms are really rigid, and you can even see an extra layer of durable material affixed to the bottom of the shoe, almost like a workman's boot. While this might be protective for hiking on a surface with rocks poking up at your feet, it's unnecessary if you're walking on a smooth road or a treadmill. That rigidity restricts your ability to roll heel to toe and makes it hard to follow proper walking form.

So try this: When you're considering a pair of shoes, hold one sneaker toe-to-heel between the palms of your hands and try to bend up the toe and heel. How much give do they have? How supple are they? If you can find shoes that are easier to bend, you'll find the heel-to-toe rolling motion easier to nail down. That's the motion that will help you walk faster.

WIGGLE YOUR TOES

One other tip about buying shoes: Have your feet measured again. Yeah, you think you've been a size 9 for your whole life? You might be in for a surprise. Over the years, our feet change in structure and size for all kinds of reasons—for instance, I found my feet were a half size bigger after two pregnancies.

Cramming your feet into shoes that are too small can create imbalances each time you take a step, and that means you'll be more likely to suffer injuries. You want to be able to wiggle your toes. Using your whole foot when you walk will help develop the muscles all over your feet and evenly distribute your weight the way nature intended.

DON'T NEGLECT THE SOCKS

While you're at it, try out different pairs of socks for walking. Forget about cotton—you need a synthetic fabric that keeps the sweat away from your feet to prevent blisters. Some socks are thin; others have extra padding that will affect the size of the sneaker you buy. So try a few, find something you like, and wear them when you're testing shoes. You might get sticker shock—socks that cost $9 or more per pair—but when you figure out how many hours you'll be wearing them, the price is well worth it.

GET STRONG!

In this stage of the Walk Your Butt Off! program, we introduce five key strength exercises that will help build muscle and firm you up. This is not purely about aesthetics. The stronger your muscles are from head to toe, the more power you will get out of each step, the better your posture will become, and the farther and faster you will walk.

The news on muscle is a little discouraging: The body loses muscle mass each year, starting in our thirties. Funny, though, how even as lean muscle decreases, our weight doesn't usually go down. Guess what that muscle is replaced with? Yep, fat. So we have to keep working at our strength routines. Cardio work doesn't do much of anything to replace the muscle we naturally lose.

For older adults, this is crucial. When people get to their golden years, their biggest problems often derive from lack of leg strength. They simply can't stand up from their chairs or may have trouble keeping their balance. You want to be building muscle early and often so you can avoid those challenges later on.

Here, Coach Michele explains the five exercises. She chose them because they'll strengthen your core, improve your posture, help develop your walking muscles, and make you faster. They're all things you can do at home, and you don't need any extra equipment, except for a doorknob to hold onto for balance. And like the speed walks, you don't want to do them on back-to-back days. Give your muscles at least one day off to recover.

Wall Press

The Wall Press uses the same movement as a pushup, but because you're vertical, your feet bear most of your body weight. This move will get you on your way to doing full pushups on the floor.

Stand arm's length away from a wall with your hands on the wall **(A)**.

Bend your elbows out to the side and bring your chest toward the wall **(B)**. It's okay if your heels come off the floor. Hold for a second, then straighten your arms. Do 15 to 20 reps.

A

B

As you get stronger, and those 15 to 20 reps feel easy, try doing these presses on lower surfaces. Over the next few weeks, progress toward a floor pushup by moving from the wall to a countertop, table (C), chair seat (no wheels on the chair, please!), and step (D). Finally, move to floor pushups (E). Be sure to use a mat for comfort on hard surfaces. Lorraine Wiedorn used the bumper of her car until she was able to do full pushups on the ground.

Plank

Lie facedown on the floor with your elbows under your shoulders and your forearms on the floor. Tuck your toes and push yourself up so you're balancing on your toes and forearms, elbows bent. Keep your abs tight and your body in line from heels to head. (Your back should be straight; you don't want your butt sticking up in the air.) Work up to holding this position for 60 seconds.

To make it easier: Try it with your knees on the floor. You can keep your feet elevated behind you or rest them on the floor, too.

Door Squats

Stand with your feet shoulder-width apart and facing the edge of an open door. Hold onto both door handles or knobs, standing close enough to keep a slight bend in your arms (A).

Using the door for balance, lean back, bend your knees, and lower yourself until your thighs are parallel to the floor. Keep your knees over your ankles and keep your abs tight (B). Stand up. Do 10 to 15 reps.

To make it easier: Don't lower quite as far (C).

To make it harder: Pause in the squat position for a count of 5.

Tabletop Leg Lift

Start on the floor on all fours. Keep your back straight and your gaze fixed on the floor about 2 feet in front of you so your head stays in line with your spine. Straighten your left leg behind you **(A)**.

A

B

With your left foot flexed, slowly lift and lower your left leg, squeezing your glutes (butt muscles) at the top of the move. Be careful not to arch your back. Keep your abs tight **(B)**. Do 10 to 15 reps with each leg.

To make it easier: Bend the knee of the leg you're lifting.

To make it harder: Extend the opposite arm of the leg you're lifting (i.e., right arm when you lift your left leg) forward while you do the move, so you're balancing on just one arm and one leg.

Bridge

A

Lie on your back with your knees bent, your feet flat on the floor, and your arms at your sides, with your palms facing up **(A)**.

Contract your abs, press into your feet, and lift your butt and lower and midback off the floor **(B)**.

Then, straighten one leg and hold it for 1 second **(C)**. Lower your foot back to the floor and then your body back to the floor. Repeat, alternating legs. Do 8 to 10 reps with each leg.

B

C

To make it easier: Keep both feet on the floor at all times and try for 15 to 20 reps.

A

To make it harder: Do one-legged bridges. Start with your right leg extended and your left leg bent, foot on the floor **(A)**. Lift your butt and lower back off the floor using your left leg only **(B)**. Do 8 to 10 reps, then switch legs.

B

SCHEDULING STRENGTH

Oh, gimme a break, you're thinking. *I'm already struggling to walk five times each week. How am I going to fit two of these strength sessions in?*

Well, let me just say that I've timed myself running through this circuit, and it takes me about 5 minutes 30 seconds. So, let's round up to 6 minutes to give you time to catch your breath between the exercises. That's the most! Twice a week, that's 12 minutes of strength training per week. I do these exercises at the landing at the top of our stairs (once I clear away the laundry basket that always seems to reside there).

I think you'll find you like the strength exercises. Sometimes, after a hard walk, when your legs and arms are really pushing, it feels good to get down on the floor and roll around on your back a little bit. It stretches you in addition to strengthening your major muscle groups.

You can do these moves at any time (just not on back-to-back days). To me, it's easiest to remember to do them immediately after a walk. You're in workout mode, your muscles are warm, and you're already sweaty and due for a shower. Get it over with. Occasionally, though, when I'm watching TV at night, I'll pop down on the floor and do a few, especially during commercials. I'm too restless to settle into my chair and sit still for an hour, so I find that doing a plank or a set of bridges in the evening works nicely.

PRIORITIES

We know this can seem overwhelming and time consuming. You're walking, thinking about your form, stretching, and now strengthening. So, let's prioritize:

1. Walk first. Aim for 5 days, but walking some is always better than doing nothing. Even if you can walk for only 10 minutes, it's better than remaining sedentary. A partial workout beats no workout.

2. If you're feeling sore, save a few minutes for stretching. You can also use gentle stretching to break up the workday. Stand up from your desk, walk briskly around "cubicle town" for 2 to 5 minutes, return to your desk, and do a little light stretching.

3. Feeling pressed for time? Two strength circuits each week is plenty. Even if you have time for only one or two of the exercises, doing some is always better than doing none.

FOOD TALK:
BREAKFAST AND HUNGER

Diet plans are everywhere. Pick the ingredient you want to load up on—dairy, meat, grapefruit—or the ingredient you want to do away with—dairy, meat, grapefruit—and you can find a diet plan and cookbook to suit your taste.

As more and more scientific research is devoted to the obesity epidemic, the findings are hard to keep up with. Which hormones control appetite? Which brain chemicals signal satiety? What role do your genes play? Are the chemicals in the lining of cans messing with our bodies? I guess this is progress, but it feels very confusing. In a 3-week stretch while the test panelists were trying the WYBO! program, I read two lengthy articles. One said you have to be "superhuman" to keep off the weight you lose. The other pointed out that weight loss is merely a matter of evaluating your habits and eating cues, such as boredom or loneliness, and reforming them. (These stories were in the same publication.)

A few weeks later, a study from Harvard made national headlines with the proclamation that red meat consumption is associated with higher mortality rates. Uh-oh. But what about that other study that said eating red meat could help lower LDL (bad cholesterol)?

It's enough to make you think the deck is stacked against you—that whether you gain or lose has nothing to do with your choices and everything to do with what's going on in your bloodstream or your subconscious.

Here's one thing all weight loss experts agree on, though: You have to eat a good breakfast.

Whew. It's something of a relief, really, at least to me. No matter what new research studies might come out, eating a substantial, well-balanced breakfast is a good strategy for your health. This simple principle is kind of like walking: Thirty minutes of walking each day is good for you. It doesn't matter what size you are, you'll be healthier if you walk. I think we can all understand that.

Breakfast is a no-brainer, too. Why is it so good for you? Eating breakfast boosts your metabolism (in other words, it increases the rate at which your body burns calories) and controls your appetite later in the day.

For proof, look at the research from the National Weight Control Registry, an 18-year-old study tracking 10,000 people who have lost at least 30 pounds and maintained the weight loss for at least a year. The results show 78 percent of those folks eat breakfast every day.

THE BEAUTY OF BREAKFAST

Chances are, if you're trying to lose weight, you're constantly attempting to consume less food. But not at breakfast. That's the beauty of this meal: If you want to lose weight, you probably have to eat *more* breakfast. How great is that?

One study published in 2012 even showed that people who ate *dessert* with breakfast lost more weight than people who had a light breakfast.

So what does an ideal breakfast look like? Here are some characteristics of that perfect meal:

- **Breakfast should be at least 300 calories.** Up to 400 calories is fine, too. A serving of Cheerios and skim milk? That's 140 calories. You need to eat more.

- **Breakfast should include at least 10 grams of protein.** The protein gives your digestive system something to work on for a few hours, so you're not tempted to stop at the doughnut cart within 45 minutes of arriving at work. Think about eggs (6 grams in one), oatmeal made with milk and sprinkled with almonds (11 total), or a breakfast sandwich with cheese and ham on a whole grain English muffin (15 total). Some cereals have more protein than others. Kashi Cinnamon Harvest has 6 grams, and with $1/2$ cup of milk, you get 4 more, so there's your 10 grams. Cornflakes, on the other hand, have only 2.

- **Breakfast is a great time to get a serving of fruits or vegetables.** In addition to being loaded with vitamins and minerals, fruits and veggies have fiber, which keeps your gut feeling full and happy and keeps the digestive system moving. Try salsa on the eggs, vegetables in the omelet, chopped apple on the oatmeal, a smoothie made with yogurt and fresh or frozen berries, or half a grapefruit.

- **Drink something.** Water, coffee, milk—don't forget to have some fluid.

- **Bring on the healthy fats.** Who said breakfast has to be fat free? A few grams of fat—12 in two eggs, for instance (140 calories), or 6 in $1/4$ cup of almonds—will help keep you feeling fuller until lunch. The fats in foods like nuts, nut butter, seeds, avocadoes, and olive oil are heart healthy. Beware the saturated version of fats, though, found in doughnuts and bacon, which may increase your risk of heart disease and diabetes.

- **Make it a meal and use utensils.** No one ever said breakfast had to be consumed while sitting in the car or standing at the kitchen counter. It's a meal just like any other. Look for foods that require you to do some chewing. Sit. Put your food on a plate. Use a spoon or a fork. You might find that devoting 10 minutes to eating your breakfast eases your stress levels at the beginning of the day.

Pop a slice of whole grain bread or an English muffin in the toaster (10 seconds).

Crack an egg into a microwavable bowl. Beat the egg (15 seconds) and put it in the microwave for 1 minute.

While the egg is cooking, section a grapefruit (45 seconds). You can prepare the grapefruit the night before, if necessary.

Total time: 2 minutes

Measure ½ cup of Quaker quick-cooking oats into a small microwavable bowl (10 seconds).

Add ½ cup of milk and stir (15 seconds).

Microwave on high for 1 minute 30 seconds.

While the oatmeal is in the microwave, chop ½ apple into bite-size pieces and count out 13 almonds; slice or crush, if desired.

Put the apple pieces and almonds on the oatmeal when it's done.

Total time: 2 minutes

Many people—our test panelists included—say that they're just not hungry when they first wake up in the morning. To which Leslie says: "Try. Try to eat within an hour of getting up." Make the change gradually. You don't have to roll out of bed and immediately sit down to a lumberjack's special. Try to eat a little earlier, add bits and pieces to your breakfast, and see how your body adapts. Test panelist Lori Powell, never a breakfast eater, worked up to having it 5 out of 7 days.

The wisdom of eating a decent breakfast is not new. And yet, many people haven't tried it. Of the 22 folks on our test panel, several weren't eating breakfast at all or were eating a few crumbs of toast. Lorraine Wiedorn was one of them but now says, "I can tell on the days I have an egg with my toast. I'm really not too hungry until lunch."

Margaret McConville

The positive: Margaret is a dedicated walker, and she followed the WYBO! program closely. Even on days when she doesn't do a formal workout, she gets plenty of exercise walking around New York City.

The problem: Margaret, 40, is a busy Manhattanite, but when she started the test panel, she was between jobs. Without work to structure her days and stressed out by unemployment, she told Leslie that her food choices were "horrible" and erratic, and she frequently ate out. "I'm an emotional eater," Margaret says.

Leslie's solution: "We talked about what *one* thing she could commit to doing, and it started with breakfast daily. Instead of the scone, muffin, or croissant from the coffee shop across the street, she agreed she would do a breakfast sandwich, oatmeal, or yogurt. I told her I want breakfast to include utensils. She laughed at first, but she said it makes sense because it makes her think about what she is eating. She will try to add protein to breakfast by making oatmeal with milk, adding a small amount of nuts or a yogurt, and she is willing to add fruit to her daily diet, with frozen berries in the winter."

The analysis: "These are small, easy, inexpensive steps Margaret can take to get started," Leslie says. "When people know they should be making better eating choices throughout the day, it can get overwhelming. So picking just one thing and starting there is a better way to go. If a person latches on to one thing to try to improve and does it with some regularity, that's great. In this case, it's breakfast. Cookie-cutter goals—like lose 10 pounds or eat 1,500 calories per day—don't work for everybody."

As far as your metabolism burn goes, having breakfast is like adding an extra log on the fire, Leslie says. You can boost your metabolism 10 percent by consistently eating breakfast. Add that up over the course of a year, and you'll notice a significant difference in your weight.

Dr. Rodney Voisine, who runs the weight loss center in Portland, Maine, tells me this is a constant drumbeat he sounds with his clients.

"We advise them that their largest meal of the day should, in fact, be breakfast," he says. "If I ask them what they had for breakfast, and they tell me they had a cheese stick and a grape, I know we've totally failed that patient. They've reverted back to the thought *If I eat less, I'll lose weight.* That's the wrong answer. I tell them: 'We need to talk. How about you have that fruit when you first get up, with some water to rehydrate, then have the cheese as part of an egg or egg white omelet with some vegetables?'"

Here's the best way to gauge your breakfast: After you eat breakfast, you should be able to stop eating for a minimum of 3 but preferably 5 hours. If you have breakfast at 7:00, hopefully you can wait until noon to eat your lunch. If you're ravenous by 9:30, you didn't eat enough.

WHEN ARE YOU HUNGRY?
WHEN ARE YOU FULL?

This discussion of breakfast—and eating enough of it to tide you over until lunch—brings us to the next principle of healthy eating: eating only when you're hungry. This is harder than it seems.

Who hasn't had the experience of eating out of boredom, sadness, stress, or frustration? I know I have. It seems like it would be an easy rule to set for yourself: Don't eat if you're not hungry. But with food so easy to get everywhere we go, it's easy to reach for snacks or second helpings without a moment's pause to evaluate what we're doing. "We are humans; we have emotions," Leslie says. "For most of us, eating is externally triggered by our environment, moods, and so on. Emotional eating is not an excuse. It is a fact."

What happens, though, is that when people use food as a way to alleviate stress or anger or whatever other unpleasant emotion they're feeling, in the end, they feel worse because they overcompensate. More unnecessary calories and one more thing to feel bad about.

On the other end is realizing when you're full, which is also harder than it sounds. A 2007 study by Brian Wansink in the journal *Obesity* showed how overweight people are more influenced by external cues of satiation (for example, they stop eating when they run out of a beverage or when the TV show they're watching has ended) than normal-weight people, who rely on internal cues, like feelings of fullness, to tell them when to stop. I have an acquaintance who has such a finely tuned sense of when she's full that she'll stop halfway through a french fry if she's had enough. Yep, she's at a healthy weight.

This week, we ask you to spend a few minutes thinking about hunger and fullness. Here are a few questions to ponder:

- How do you know when you're hungry? What happens inside your body?
- Do you eat when you're hungry?
- Do you eat when you're not hungry?
- How do you know when you're full? What happens inside your body?

Leslie counsels many clients each year who struggle with their weight, and they often describe scenarios like the ones listed below. Our test panelists talked about their difficulties with hunger and fullness, too. See if any (or more than one) fit you:

- **Constant nosher:** You eat so frequently that you never know what it is to feel any kind of hunger pangs.
- **Too busy to notice:** Your days are nonstop and pressure packed. Lunch is impossible, and you don't really notice if you're hungry.

When you finally do sit down to a meal, you feel ravenous and over-eat as a result.

- **Hungry eyes:** You're motivated to eat by things you see in your environment, like the cupcakes a coworker brought to the office. Even though you just ate lunch and aren't hungry at all, you have to have one. Or you walk by the bakery when the bread is baking or see a commercial for food on TV, and you're off in search of something to eat.

- **Emotional eater:** You eat in response to psychological stimulus—you've had a good day, a bad day, a frustrating day, a boring day, or a stressful day, and you want certain foods in response to that.

- **Habitual eater:** You eat out of routine. At night, you always watch a certain TV show with a particular snack whether or not you're hungry.

- **Reward eater:** I walked 4 miles today, therefore I deserve to eat this dessert. And that one, too.

- **Clean-plate club:** I'm stuffed to the gills, but there's more food on the plate, so I have to finish it.

Any of those seem like you? More than one?

Pick one to focus on this week. Remember, you're not going to fix months and years of dodgy eating in a week's time. It takes months and years to put the weight on, so it can take that long to reverse the trend. Start by examining your habits. Think of one change you can realistically focus on and try to make that change habitual. If you can stop yourself just once this week from eating when you're not hungry, from eating past the point of fullness, or from eating out of anger or stress, you're on the right track.

To-Do List

☐ Take a look at your calendar to plan at least five times you can walk during the next week.

☐ Complete at least five workouts, including at least 2 brisk walks and 3 speed walks. Don't schedule speed walks on back-to-back days.

☐ Try the strength exercises. See how long they take you (should be about 6 minutes) and figure out when you have time to do them at least twice each week but not on back-to-back days.

☐ Go to the supermarket to buy the ingredients you need for a healthy breakfast. Make sure your breakfast has enough total calories and protein. Try to include fluid and a serving of a fruit or vegetable. Do you have time to eat it? Are you full until lunch?

☐ Think before you eat: "Am I really hungry?"
Ask yourself as you're eating: "Am I full yet?"

Steve Cobb -

Age: 43

Height: 5'9"

Total pounds lost:
11.4 pounds
in 12 weeks

Total inches lost:
9½ inches,
**including 4 inches
from his waist**

Starting walk time:
15:28

Ending walk time:
12:39

Faster by:
2 minutes
49 seconds

Before

PUT SOME MUSCLE IN IT

Day job: I work in information technology for a bank, and I'm married with two young kids.

How I got here: I've battled depression and anxiety since high school. For years, my physician urged me to exercise, but it's very easy to lie on the couch and let the gray cloud hang over your head. In college, I played volleyball and soccer (I was a goalie). I always enjoyed sports and considered myself athletic, but all that jumping took a toll on my lower back.

How I started: I wasn't doing anything before joining the test panel. There was a time when bending over to tie my shoes in the morning was a challenge. I did the walks, mostly in the morning and on the treadmill. I did have to talk myself out of bed. I'd set the alarm for 6 a.m., hit snooze a couple of times, and then get going.

What I've noticed: I've felt more energetic. The walks are a pick-me-up. I still drink my coffee, but going into work the morning after a walk, I feel more alert, more pumped, more ready for the day. When I was lying around and not exercising, I had brain fog, a tougher time concentrating. Exercise makes me more alert, which helps me deal with the times of anxiety. I don't know that I'll ever be able to eradicate my depression and anxiety issues. But the exercise is a tool I can use to help me deal with them.

Winning strategies: I've tried to forgo second helpings. And my sweets—chocolate anvd cookies—I've tried to cut back. I think that I now know when I'm full, when I'm no longer hungry. I don't just eat because it tastes good or allow myself to get painfully stuffed after the meal. I've definitely become much more conscious of that.

Workout mind-set: I consider 4.0 miles per hour to be my brisk pace and 4.6 to be my fast walking speed. I like the speed walks with the fast intervals a little better than the steady-paced walks. Intervals make the workout go faster, the workout is a little more interesting, and those are the workouts where I get that endorphin kick. I did a 5-K on New Year's Eve with the group, and my time was 42:18, which works out to 13:38 per mile.

Healthy signals: I like the sweat. That means I'm doing something. It makes me feel good.

Best advice: I think walking is a great way to get into exercise, especially for people who have some injuries that keep them from running. You can turn walking into rigorous exercise. People look at it like, "Oh, gee, you walk. That doesn't sound very substantial." If you go at it hard, it certainly can be very vigorous. So I'd tell people: Don't write it off. Walking is very serious and a great way to exercise.

I think it's critical you become more aware of what you put in your body. I didn't even think about it before. That's an important first step. I used to think healthy eating was all salads, but now I know what it means to have a well-balanced diet.

CHAPTER 5

THE
HEALING
Power of
Sweat

Do you sweat when you walk? I hope so. You should be sweating.

Sweat is a good sign. It's firm evidence—well, maybe *liquid evidence* is more accurate—that you're pushing your body and working hard, and in response, your body is cooling itself off. Perspiration means that you're reaching the right level of intensity. Not sweating? You're too comfortable.

"Oh, I sweat like a pig," Arlene Scott told me. Even in the middle of the winter, she would head outside for her walks in little more than a shirt and a windbreaker, and within 3 minutes, the perspiration would be forming on her forehead. A few minutes later, the windbreaker would be tied around her waist. Me, I need more like 7 minutes before I start to glisten, but maybe that's because our basement, where we keep the treadmill, is a little chilly.

Get used to sweating. Embrace it. Prepare for it. Before you walk, especially on your speed walk days, change into clothes you don't mind getting sweaty. You're an athlete now, and that's what athletes do. They sweat, and they dress for sweat. Prepare for extra laundry, too. In fact, my husband exiled my workout clothes to their own little laundry basket and their own load in the wash. He claims this laundry segregation keeps the rest of the family's street clothes smelling fresh. (I think his nose is a little oversensitive, but as long as he gives me time to walk and run, I'm not going to argue.)

I once interviewed CNN's medical correspondent, Dr. Sanjay Gupta, for an article in *Runner's World*. This is a busy guy: He's on TV a lot and a practicing neurosurgeon when the cameras aren't rolling. I'll always remember one thing he said during that interview: "I try and break a sweat every day."

See? Doctor's orders.

If you haven't noticed yourself sweating yet, get ready for it with the workout in this stage—you'll find it on page 101. In the meanwhile, let me tell you how this stage is different from what you've done so far.

A NEW TWIST

In this week's workouts, we introduce a new component: the challenge walk. This replaces one of your speed walks, so you're still doing a minimum of five workouts this week.

Here's how to do the challenge walk:

- Warm up for 5 minutes. (Start at an easy pace for the first 2 minutes, then shift to a brisk pace for the next 3 minutes.)

- Then walk as fast as you can for 10 minutes, noting where you start and where you finish. Turn around and walk back to the start at a more comfortable pace. Repeat each week, using the same route, noting how much farther you can walk in 10 minutes.

- It's best to do these walks on level paved terrain or on a track or treadmill.

Total walk time is *at least* 25 minutes. It's tough to tell exactly because your return trip after the hard 10 minutes will be slower than it was on the way out. (If you're able to cover the same distance in 10 minutes on the way back, you weren't walking fast enough for the first 10 minutes.)

The important component of this workout is completing it in the same location week after week. That way, you can measure your progress. You'll get a visible sign of how you're improving by how far you can go in 10 minutes. So make sure to keep track of which house you start at, or which telephone pole, or which line on the track. Do the same with the finish and write it down so you can make an accurate comparison in a week. If you're on the treadmill, be sure to make a note of what the distance is when you start and when you finish. On a treadmill or track, when you're done with the "challenge" portion, be sure to walk that same distance at a slower pace so you match the workout distance that the outdoor, point-to-point walkers are going. Don't skip it!

Bethany Lee got this. She did her challenge walks on a trail in Bethlehem, Pennsylvania, which heads toward a bridge that passes overhead. Every week, she'd get a little bit closer to that bridge. "I am so close and yet so far," she told me. When we did a 5-K walk together—a New Year's Eve road race with more than 600 runners and walkers—she pointed it out. "See? That's the bridge I'm aiming for." She kept her eyes on the prize.

It's important to set small goals on the way to larger ones. If the goal is to lose 40 pounds or walk a 10-K, that might take awhile, and anyone could get discouraged on the journey. With the challenge walk, you get instant feedback, a weekly goal to shoot for.

Elite athletes struggle with this all the time, too. Nicole Blood, a national-class 5000-meter runner, blogged about the frustrations of regaining fitness after an injury and her progress in the buildup to the 2012 Olympic track-and-field trials. "Take one week at a time," she wrote. "Don't compare yourself to anyone but the athlete you were the day before. Are you stronger? Faster? More confident? Good. Then you're moving forward. And that's all that matters."

The challenge walks will be evidence of how the athlete you are today is different from the one you were last week. Oh, and one more thing: As you'll see in the following workout, the speed walks get harder this week, as they do every week. (Now the fast-paced walking time exceeds the brisk-paced walking time.)

The steady, brisk walks change, too. Instead of a minimum of 20 minutes, we ask you to push the minimum to 30 minutes. Thus, you're making changes in every workout this week.

A few more notes about the challenge walk. Because it's a "hard" day, just like the speed walk workout, try not to do it back-to-back with

WALK YOUR BUTT OFF!

STAGE 5

Minimum: 5 walks
Strength workouts*: 2–3 times this week

2 TO 4 BRISK WALKS

After warming up by walking at an easy pace for 2 to 3 minutes, you should walk at a purposeful pace, as if you need to get to an appointment, about 3 to 4 mph, for 30 to 40 minutes. Do a minimum of 2 brisk walks this week; a maximum of 4 if you're trying to walk every day.

Total workout time: 22–33 minutes

2 SPEED WALKS

➤ Start with a 2-minute warm-up at an easy pace.

➤ Then do 1 minute at a brisk pace and 1 minute 30 seconds at a fast pace 8 times.

➤ End with 3 minutes of easy walking.

Total fast walking time: 12 minutes.
Total workout time: 25 minutes.

1 CHALLENGE WALK

➤ Start with a 5-minute warm-up (2 minutes easy, 3 minutes brisk).

➤ Then do 10 minutes as fast as you can, noting your starting point and finishing point or distance.

➤ Return and walk back to the start at a more comfortable pace.

Total workout time: At least 25 minutes

For the strength workout, see page 75.

another speed walk. Instead, give yourself a day off or a day of brisk walking in between.

Second, you probably think you can go as fast for the hard 10 minutes of the challenge walk as you do during the speed intervals on your speed walk days. Don't worry if you can't keep up that pace. It's natural to go a little slower because you're not getting any breaks. Just do the best you can. And if you find that you've set a pace that's a little too ambitious and you feel yourself slowing down after the first 5 minutes, don't fret about that either. For the first week, you simply want to set a baseline. Next week, you work on improving that baseline. The Technique Tip below will help you with your speed. All these Technique Tips will help your stride generate more power so you go faster. You are not walking incorrectly if you can't remember them all. Practice them little by little until they feel natural. You might want to spend time during each brisk walk telling yourself, *Okay, for the next 3 minutes I'm going to think about pushing off the ground.* Then do it again for 3 minutes later in the walk. Don't overthink it, though. Remember to keep moving without getting so bogged down in form that you neglect the exercise.

TECHNIQUE TIP #4

• Push off strong

After you roll from your heel to your toes, focus on really pushing off the ground to propel yourself forward. For maximum power, bend at the ball of your foot, raising the back of your foot as if you were trying to show the person behind you the sole of your shoe.

HOW DO I KNOW HOW FAST I'M GOING?

If you want a ballpark estimate on your speed, you can use the charts below. They're not exact, but they will give you a pretty good idea. All you have to do is count your steps for 1 minute, both left and right. Or you can count your steps for 30 seconds and multiply by 2. Then find your height, look across the row for the step count closest to yours, and look at the top of the column to find your speed. These charts come from a 2008 study by W. W. K. Hoeger published in the American College of Sports Medicine's *Health & Fitness Journal*.

Women

SPEED	2.5 MPH	3 MPH	3.5 MPH	4.0 MPH	4.6 MPH
HEIGHT					
5'0"	109	119	128	137	148
5'2"	108	117	127	135	146
5'4"	107	116	125	133	144
5'6"	106	114	123	131	142
5'8"	105	113	122	129	140
5'10"	103	111	120	127	137
6'0"	102	110	118	125	135

Men

SPEED	2.5 MPH	3 MPH	3.5 MPH	4.0 MPH	4.6 MPH
HEIGHT					
5'6"	104	113	121	129	139
5'8"	103	111	120	127	137
5'10"	102	109	118	125	135
6'0"	101	108	116	123	133
6'2"	100	107	115	121	131
6'4"	99	106	113	120	128

Our test panelists enjoyed this. Counting steps for a minute is a good way to break up a workout, to see that you're at the proper intensity, or to compete with yourself. It's a signpost in a workout that might not be measured any other way, and some people need that. "When Michele first had us count our steps, I was like, 'Yeah, I can do this,'" says Val Donohue (who stands 6 feet tall). "I'm very competitive with myself. The first time I counted was like 120. As soon as I had a number attached to it, I was like, 'Okay, now I want to break that number. Gotta beat that number.' Then, when I started learning about proper technique and the shorter, faster steps, it was closer to 135. My heart was pounding out of my chest."

ABOUT THAT TREADMILL

Some folks on our panel walked exclusively on the treadmill. That's a fine choice. A treadmill saves exercisers from having to worry about weather, traffic, dogs, or any other outdoor hazards. If you've got small children in the house, you can work out on a treadmill when they're sleeping without leaving the house.

The primary detriment of treadmills is that people become obsessed with what the numbers on the console read. They beat themselves up if they don't walk as fast on Thursday as they did on Tuesday. Or worse, they limit themselves. They think, *I'm leaving that treadmill at 4.2 mph; that's the best I can possibly do*, when in reality, if they were walking outdoors without a number staring them in the face, they could walk a lot faster.

So here's what Coach Michele has to say about treadmills: They're great tools. They keep you honest and make it easier to work out. But don't let the numbers trick you into walking slower than you're able or get you discouraged. In fact, sometimes it's better for your brain if you cover the console with a towel—at least the part that shows the speed. That way you can walk by feel, not by what the red digital display tells you.

And if you can't resist staring at the numbers? When you're doing your fast segments, try to push it up one tick faster on the final interval. Don't let the treadmill get you stuck in a rut.

A BUFFER ZONE

If you have been doing only the minimum suggested amount of walking, keep in mind that with this stage's workout, you have to allot 20 more minutes each week for the brisk walks. This might require another look at your calendar to ensure you have that time. Or you might need to rearrange your speed walk days and brisk walk days, giving yourself more time for the brisk walks.

If possible, make sure you give yourself a full 30 minutes for walking, plus whatever other time you need on the front end—for getting changed, for psyching yourself up, for filling your water bottle—and on the back end—for getting ready to re-enter life indoors. (It's nice to have a little postworkout buffer zone so you're not feeling like you're always running late to your next commitment.) A 30-minute walk might require 45 minutes out of your day.

It can be tough to find time for that buffer zone. I'm constantly pushing the envelope, walking into my son's school to get him with the sweat dripping into my eyes. But I attempt to add at least 15 minutes on the back end of every workout for stretching, showering, and just taking a deep breath. It makes the workout more enjoyable, knowing I don't have to rush through it to get immediately to the next thing. In the end, that buffer zone often shrinks to nothing, but when it's there, I'm less stressed. I've had a chance to complete my workout—and make the transition back into the real world.

FOOD TALK:

A REAL SERVING SIZE

About 5 weeks into the test panel, I was speaking to one of the participants, who confessed that something was bothering her. "I'm getting off the treadmill after my brisk walk, and the thing tells me I burned 133 calories," she complained. "All that work and sweat for 30 minutes and all I burn is 133 calories?"

Well, yes and no. Treadmill calorie counters are not all that accurate. If you have to key in your weight when you start your workout, they're a little closer, but don't take the digital display as gospel.

On the other hand, it's true that these early workouts aren't major calorie-torchers. You'll burn somewhere in the neighborhood of 200 calories after a 30-minute fast walk or 40-minute brisk walk.

Which doesn't mean you shouldn't walk. Remember what Dr. Blair's research has proven: For longevity, health, and well-being, it's better to be overweight and active than thin and sedentary. A hugely popular YouTube video, titled *23½ Hours*, made the rounds in 2011 and 2012, with more than 2 million views. In it, a Canadian doctor says that exercise makes the single biggest difference in your health and that physicians should be prescribing it more. If exercise is a medicine, what's the dose? Thirty minutes a day.

But when you're trying to shed pounds—and we know you are—those calorie totals can seem pretty skimpy.

Fear not. The workouts in the next chapter will get even more challenging, and as a result, you'll be burning more. But the reality is, for weight loss, you need to keep close tabs on your eating, too. Remember, weight loss happens faster when you work on both sides of the calorie equation at the same time: the calories you burn (more) and the calories you consume (less). It's a lot easier and faster to eliminate an unnecessary, high-calorie snack like soda or chips than it is to get out there and walk for 30 minutes.

PAY ATTENTION TO PORTIONS

Another quick and easy way to slash a few calories is to pay attention to portions. By eating beyond a serving size—sometimes *way* beyond, like double or triple a serving size—you're sabotaging your healthy-eating efforts, often unknowingly.

When you kept a food log back in Week 2, we asked you to record only *what*, *where*, and *when* you ate and drank. At this stage of the program, you can make a lot of additional progress toward your weight loss goals by paying attention to *how much* you're eating.

How can you do this? By reading, measuring, and learning.

This is not to say you need to drive yourself crazy tallying your daily calories. You can track your calories if you want to, and there are plenty of apps and Web sites to help you do that. My personal favorite is CalorieKing.com. But this isn't necessary.

What *is* necessary is having a ballpark estimate, to know roughly how many calories are in certain foods. If you go overboard eating carrots, no harm done. If you go way over on salad dressing, that's a different story. Four tablespoons instead of 2 could mean 280 calories instead of 140. In other words, those 20 minutes you walked on the treadmill? You just put those calories right back on—and on your salad, no less.

DETECTIVE WORK

Time to play food detective. First step, read the labels on boxes and containers to figure out what a serving size is. This amount differs among brands. Take cereal, for instance: A serving of granola is a lot smaller than a serving of Cheerios. And a serving of ice cream is ½ cup, which is not very much.

Second, get ready to measure. "Our eyes are notoriously unreliable at judging how much food we're eating," Leslie says. You think you know what a ½ cup serving of ice cream is? Test yourself. Serve what you think is ½ cup, then measure a true ½ cup. How did you do?

Get out your measuring cups and spoons and leave them on the counter so you remember to use them. If you don't have any, you can purchase cheap ones at a dollar store or at any discount store.

Measure the serving sizes of the foods you eat frequently so you begin to learn what they look like. If I splurge on the country wheat bread, each slice has 130 calories versus the 60 calories in a slice of thin bread I regularly buy. So when I do that, I hold the cheese. I actually count almonds because they're such a high-calorie food. The serving size, ¼ cup, fits 26 almonds, so I put half that on my oatmeal in the morning. Call me crazy.

Here are the foods where people tend to go way beyond a serving size without realizing it:

- **Cereal, pasta, and rice.** Some brands of pasta don't make it easy for you. For example, one serving of Barilla's spaghetti is one-eighth of a box. Great, how much is that? Gotta divide a box into equal eighths first?

- **Peanut butter, cream cheese, mayo, and salad dressing.** For salad dressing, try measuring out the 2 tablespoons. For the others, try to make sure you can still see the bread or bagel peeking through after you've spread them.

- **Speaking of bagels and muffins . . .** Are you eating a New York–style bagel, with a 4-inch diameter, or something closer to a hockey puck (3 inches across and 1 inch thick)?

- **Juice.** A recommended serving size is usually either 4 or 6 ounces, so try measuring that and filling the rest of the cup with water or seltzer to make the cup look full.

- **Snack foods such as crackers, pretzels, and nuts.** Count them or measure them first instead of eating them straight from the package.

- **Sweets such as ice cream and frozen yogurt, and brownies in a pan.** Find a small cup, like a cappuccino cup, for ice cream. For baked goods, cut one for yourself, then sit and savor it. Put the rest in the freezer or get them out of the house.

GO AHEAD AND HAVE MORE

This exercise in measuring your food is supposed to be about education, not deprivation. The recommended serving size of pasta is often ½ cup. If you want to eat more, that's understandable. But maybe you can cut back to 1½ servings instead of your typical 2 or 3 servings. Compromise a little.

You can also experiment with different brands. One kind of bread might be a calorie bomb, so try a wrap instead. Or you might be surprised by how *much* you can eat. Deli turkey is only 22 calories per slice, so go ahead and stack four slices on your sandwich.

"The purpose of doing this is to get your eyes familiar with it," Leslie says. "A serving size looks different than what we normally eat, and we want to learn what a true serving size looks like."

PRO TIPS FOR PERFECT PORTIONS

If you realize your portions have been all out of whack and you're trying to cut back, try these tips:

- **The ideal size of a dinner plate is 8 to 9 inches.** Most American plates are larger. I go no farther than my cupboard to find evidence of this, as the plates my husband and I registered for when we got married are 11 inches. (They're so big that the dishwasher arm can't really rotate smoothly when they're in there.) If you have giant-plate syndrome, try eating off a salad plate. Or if you're at the dollar store, purchase a smaller plate, bowl, and cup so the smaller food amounts don't look so puny. Same with your fork. Use a salad fork, which holds slightly less, so you're not cramming large bites into your mouth at one time.

- **Try trimming just a little from what you normally serve yourself.** Take a bit off the edges. Then it's okay to clean your plate. And you'll gradually get used to a smaller serving size rather than knocking your portions in half the first week you try this.

- **Don't go family style.** Leave the food in the kitchen, fix yourself a plate, then go sit down. Use the dining room, if possible. It's just so tempting to serve yourself larger helpings or seconds when the food is on the table, staring you in the face.

- **Cook a little less.** Instead of the whole box of pasta, prepare two-thirds of it. Then half. Then you don't have to worry so much about portions.

- **At restaurants, ask for what you want.** Eat an appetizer as your entrée, split an entrée with a dining companion, or get half of it bagged before it comes to the table. Your server shouldn't bat an eyelash. If he or she does, go somewhere else next time. But you can still enjoy restaurant eating and keep the portions under control. You don't have to be in the "land of no" all the time, Leslie points out. You can be in the "land of a little less" or the "land of swaps."

Hopefully, this experience will be eye opening. Take a few moments and write down what you've learned. Examples:

When I eat a ½ cup serving of ice cream, it comes just below the line on the juice glasses.

The restaurant in town makes omelets exactly to order—one egg, one egg white—and when I asked for one spoonful of home fries, that's what I got.

_____

_____

_____

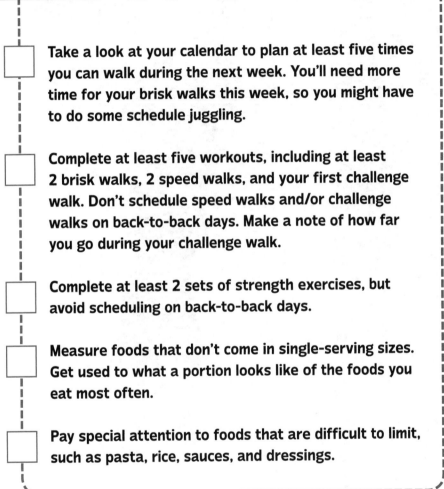

CHAPTER 5 ▶ To-Do List

☐ Take a look at your calendar to plan at least five times you can walk during the next week. You'll need more time for your brisk walks this week, so you might have to do some schedule juggling.

☐ Complete at least five workouts, including at least 2 brisk walks, 2 speed walks, and your first challenge walk. Don't schedule speed walks and/or challenge walks on back-to-back days. Make a note of how far you go during your challenge walk.

☐ Complete at least 2 sets of strength exercises, but avoid scheduling on back-to-back days.

☐ Measure foods that don't come in single-serving sizes. Get used to what a portion looks like of the foods you eat most often.

☐ Pay special attention to foods that are difficult to limit, such as pasta, rice, sauces, and dressings.

Age: 39

Height: 6'0"

Total pounds lost:
7.6 pounds
in 12 weeks

Total inches lost:
10½ inches,
**including 1¾ inches
from her hips and
1 inch from her waist**

Starting walk time:
14:14

Ending walk time:
12:30

Faster by:
1 minute
44 seconds

Val Donohue

Before

Day job: I'm a nurse and a women's college basketball coach, married, with one son.

How I got here: The winter, with basketball season, is my busiest time. I've always gained weight over the winter and lost weight over the summer. Before my son was born 9 years ago, I would fluctuate 15 pounds from summer to winter, but even at my heaviest, I was at a healthy weight. Now my weight swings by 30 pounds, and my lowest weight is still too high. I'm either gaining 2 pounds a week for months or losing 2 pounds a week for months. There's no middle ground, and I'm trying to break that.

I sabotage myself with an all-or-nothing mentality. Either I'm working out and eating perfectly or I'm not doing anything and I'm eating terribly. It's always been like "I haven't worked out for a day or two. What's one more day?" And I'll eat 3,000 calories in a sitting. The worst part is that I'm a nurse. I know better.

How I started: Being on the test panel helped me see that even 20 minutes of walking is better than nothing. I've learned to pack my work clothes, drive to work, and then do my walk, because once I set foot in the office or turn on the computer, I'll never get my workout in. It's funny; my boss has adopted the same strategy. She trained to run a half-marathon by parking near work and doing her runs, then coming into the office.

Winning strategies: Once I get fatigued, my ability to make good decisions goes out the window. After the game, you're stressed, even if you win. The team stops at Wawa (a local convenience store) on the way home, about 9:30 at night. If I'm there during the day, I can get the fruit cup and the salad. Turn that into night, I'm exhausted, and I'll end up with the family-size Turtle Chex Mix.

Now even if I'm not ordering perfectly, I'll do it in moderation.

If I have a sandwich, I'll just get water with it.

I'm trying to be better about planning through the day. Eating breakfast is huge for me. If I don't, I'm starved midafternoon, and I have no control when I go to get something for lunch. Now I eat something that has protein and carbohydrates and fiber, and then I make sure I eat again within 4 hours. I try to stock my fridge at work with Healthy Choice meals and yogurts.

Workout mind-set: With my all-or-nothing mentality, I was either running or doing nothing. I didn't look at walking as an exercise. That has changed. Once Michele adjusted my form and I could really go fast, my heart was really pumping on the speed walks.

Big win: Seven pounds does not feel like much, and I know I have a long way to go. But normally, as the basketball season ends, I'm heavier by 30 pounds, so in a way, I feel like I'm 37 pounds ahead of where I was this time last year. And my postseason runs have been better than usual. My first time out, I normally make it 2 minutes, max. But after walking all winter, I was able to run comfortably for 13 minutes. Then I stopped and walked the rest of the way.

CHAPTER 6

Pushing
THE
Pace

One of the most miraculous things about the human body is how easily it adapts to the stress of exercise.

And one of the most *frustrating* things about the human body is how easily it adapts to the stress of exercise.

Start a walking program when you haven't been active, and you'll feel taxed, tired, and probably a little sore. You've probably noticed, though, that if you keep at it, by about the second week, walking seems easy.

To continue improving your fitness and to nudge the body into relinquishing some pounds, you need to mix it up. Some days are short and fast; some days are longer and slower (the challenge comes from the length, not the speed). Uphills and downhills of varying inclines and lengths are a way to keep it fresh; so are strength training and walking in warmer temperatures. In other words, you have to keep your body guessing. You want to surprise it, challenge it, prevent it from getting too comfortable in its routine.

Sure, 30 minutes of even slow walking wards off a host of health problems. Any movement is better than no movement. Even at gentle to moderate levels, exercise is hugely protective medicine.

But if you're striving to be in better physical condition, do more, lose more weight, and feel stronger and more energetic, your exercise routine has to change as you get into shape. If you keep repeating the same exercises, you'll get into a rut or hit a plateau (pick your own geological metaphor) and simply stop improving.

That's part of the reason Coach Michele's program inserted those challenge walks in Stage 5 and why the speed walks keep getting harder. As you mix up your workouts and crank up the intensity every week, your body is tested in new and different ways. In other words, you're getting in shape.

FLAT OR HILLS?

When you walk uphill, you need to shorten your steps and use your muscles a little differently than you do on flat ground. Uphill walking is great for the glutes, and strengthening those muscles in the butt will make you faster for your speed walks. Hills also help you feel the push-off as your foot rolls heel to toe with each step.

Inclines stimulate your cardiovascular system, too; they help get your lungs working and your heart pumping. They also help keep things interesting. When the terrain changes, it gives the workout a new look.

For the speed walks, though, it's best to stick to level ground if at all possible. Because you're trying to really push the pace during those workouts, you don't need the added test of a hill. When you use a consistently flat course for walking fast, you'll get a better sense of your progress. It's tougher to gauge your improvement if the incline is changing at the same time as your pace.

Same goes for treadmill walkers. It's fine to bump up the incline when you're walking at a steady rate on a brisk walk. Doing so can help pass the time. I've always been a fan of 2-minute hills: 10 seconds to let the treadmill rise up into position and then 2 minutes at about 3.5 percent incline. Return to level, walk for 5 minutes, then throw in another 2-minute hill. You'll be blasting through 30 minutes before you can get bored. But for the speed walks, leave the incline button alone.

In the meantime, here's the Stage 6 workout, with another challenge walk. Be sure to do it in the same location as last week so you can see if you made any improvement. It's worth noting if you make it even a few steps farther.

When you consider the speed walks and the challenge walk together, you're doing 40 minutes of fast walking with the Stage 6 workout. That's a lot of speed. So how do you get faster? You probably think longer strides are the key, but in fact, that's not the case. Check out the Technique Tip below.

This suggestion probably seems counterintuitive, but give it a try. Those shorter steps will make you walk smoother instantly; I know it has worked for me. I remember watching one of the petite members of our test panel, Jennifer Durham, walking, and it seemed like her legs were a blur during her speed intervals. She covered some ground, that's for sure. For several other test panelists, hearing that they should shorten their stride made a world of difference in their ability to walk fast.

TECHNIQUE TIP #5

• Take short, quick steps

Shorter, quicker steps are the key to going faster. One of the most common mistakes people make when trying to walk faster is *over-striding*. They reach their front leg out farther than normal. Instead of speeding you along, big steps actually slow you down because it's harder to get your body weight over an outstretched leg. In a sense, your leg acts as a break. When you take steps that are too long, you have a choppy stride and you actually increase the impact of each step, which in turn may boost your risk for injury. Shorter, quicker steps allow for a smooth, rolling stride, and they make it easier for you to shift your body weight over your front leg and swing your back leg forward. The result: a faster walking speed.

WALK YOUR BUTT OFF!

STAGE 6

Minimum: 5 walks
Strength workouts*: 2–3 times this week

2 TO 4 BRISK WALKS

After warming up by walking at an easy pace for 2 to 3 minutes, you should walk at a purposeful pace, as if you need to get to an appointment, about 3 to 4 mph, for 30 to 40 minutes. Do a minimum of 2 brisk walks this week; a maximum of 4 if you're trying to walk every day.

Total workout time: 32–43 minutes

2 SPEED WALKS

➤ Start with a 2-minute warm-up at an easy pace.
➤ Then do 1 minute at a brisk pace and 2 minutes 30 seconds at a fast pace 6 times.
➤ End with 3 minutes of easy walking.

Total fast walking time: 15 minutes.
Total workout time: 26 minutes.

1 CHALLENGE WALK

➤ Start with a 5-minute warm-up (2 minutes easy, 3 minutes brisk).
➤ Then do 10 minutes as fast as you can, noting your starting point and finishing point or distance.
➤ Return and walk back to the start at a more comfortable pace.

Total workout time: At least 25 minutes

For the strength workout, see page 75.

WHAT IF I MISS A WORKOUT?

Life happens. You wake up with the stomach flu, your child wakes up with the stomach flu, your client calls from Tokyo at 11 p.m. and wants an update on the numbers. The alarm goes off the next morning, and exercise loses out to the siren song of the pillow.

Sometimes, you have to miss your workout. Don't beat yourself up about it.

Then there's the inner voice that makes you miss the workout. The one that tells you how tired you are, how you'd better fold the laundry instead, how it's too cold or too hot, or oh, what the hell, you can do it tomorrow.

We all slip from time to time. The important thing is to catch ourselves before we fall. That means getting back into a routine as soon as possible. Occasional slips aren't going to hinder your results; scientific research has even proven this. It's when we think that one slip is the end of the world and stop making the effort that we fall and end up back where we started.

If you do have to miss several workouts in a row—for illness or injury—it would be foolish to try to jump back into the routine in the exact same place you left. Instead, go back two (or more) stages earlier and pick it up from there. There's no deadline on completing the program, and you need to cut your body some slack as you recover from your ailments.

FOOD TALK:
THE POWER OF PROTEIN AND LUNCH

Look back at the blockbuster diets of years past, and they're founded on a high-protein, low-carb philosophy: the Atkins Diet, the Paleo Diet, the Dukan Diet.

STAT SHEET

Age: 54

Total weight lost:
1 pound

Total inches lost:
4 inches,
including more
than 2 inches
from her thighs

Walk time: Faster by
*2 minutes
8 seconds*

Donna Karoly

Big wins: "I've gotten into a good routine of going to the gym on Monday, Tuesday, Thursday, and Saturday mornings. I found I challenge myself more if I'm on a treadmill. And I can do a plank now. When I get home from the gym, I find I'm more relaxed. I'm not picking at anyone or at any food. I'm also sleeping much better at night, not snoring, and not waking up. It used to be I'd get night sweats and then I'd be up for at least an hour. I'm sleeping much more soundly now."

Spreading the word: Donna organized a building-wide walk at her company—a few laps around the outside of the building—as part of Customer Service Week. The exercise was a big hit, and it helped the employees reconnect with each other.

Next steps: "I'd like to lose more weight, and I still find getting enough protein is tough. I'm trying: I'll have a quick veggie omelet in the morning now, and on weekends, I'll try to cook two dinners for the week. But it is a work in progress."

Protein, protein, protein. Carbs are ostracized, sent to the margins, where only the marathoners and naturally thin people can indulge. Pasta and bagels are pushed to the side of the grocery aisles to make room for . . . high-protein pasta and higher-protein varieties of bagels.

So, are the creators of these diets right? Is protein the miracle cure for slimming down and toning up?

Well, like anything else, Americans have a habit of taking advice and manipulating it to justify their eating habits. Not all protein is created equal. Sure, there might be 25 grams of protein in that Big Mac, but it comes along with 540 calories and 29 grams of fat. And if you add a side of french fries and a Coke, well, your protein comes at a very high cost.

Ultimately, to lose weight, you need to take in fewer calories than you burn, whether they're protein, carbohydrate, or fat.

Let's keep it simple: Protein can be helpful for weight loss, because it makes you feel fuller. A 2011 study from the University of Missouri demonstrated that people who ate high-protein meals, consumed in three eating occasions throughout the day (instead of six), reported a lower late-night desire to eat and less preoccupation with thoughts of food.

What's more, it takes great effort for your digestive system to get protein through the gut and into the bloodstream, so you burn more calories while you're digesting protein. And protein helps build muscle, maintain joints and ligaments, build bone and teeth, and so on.

But if you think you can eat sausage for breakfast, bacon for lunch, and burgers for dinner just because it's protein, you probably won't see much besides higher cholesterol and a bigger number on the scale. With protein, it's the same as everything else: Avoid the all-or-nothing approach and remember: There are no quick fixes.

That said, most of us still don't get enough protein. How much is enough?

LESLIE'S LAW

To figure out how much protein you need in a day, take your ideal body weight and divide it by 2. That's the number of grams of protein you need. For example, if your ideal weight is 150 pounds, you need 75 grams of protein in a day.

This is another number you don't want to interpret too literally; you just want to be in the ballpark. If you're aiming for 75 grams, and one day you get 65 and the next day you get 80, you're doing just fine. Too many of us fall far short of our target protein amounts.

SPREAD THE WEALTH

You also aren't doing yourself any favors if you get just a few grams of protein early in the day and then sit down at night to a giant slab of meat. The body would rather get it in equal increments all day long, some at every eating occasion, whether a snack or a meal. That way, you get the hunger-squelching effects and the metabolism boost throughout the day, not right before bed.

If you're not eating these foods already, consider giving them a try for their protein:

Beans

Soy foods

Low-fat dairy: skim milk, Greek yogurt, and cottage cheese; and portion-controlled cheeses like slices, Laughing Cow wedges, and string cheese

Eggs

Poultry

Fish

Shellfish

Lean meat

Grains, such as quinoa or pastas and wraps with extra protein added

Grocery staples, such as bread, cereal, and pasta, that come in protein-enhanced forms (Read the labels carefully, and make sure added protein doesn't come packed with extra sugar and calories.)

INSURANCE POLICY

Another option if you're having trouble getting the protein you need is either vanilla or unflavored whey protein isolate. It can be added to any liquid or soft food, like a smoothie, oatmeal, soup, or vegetable juice. It's about 100 calories per ounce, but it packs 23 grams of protein.

LOG AGAIN

At this point in the program, if you haven't been continuously logging your food intake, take a few days to keep another food log. As you did during Stage 1, log for at least 3 days (longer if you want) and write down everything you eat. Try to include a weekend day. We have included space for you to do this in the workbook on pages 262–264.

We're asking you to pay attention to two additional questions this time, so you'll notice the Stage 6 Food Log is slightly different from the first one you kept. Here's a sample:

WALK YOUR BUTT OFF! *Food Log*

DATE 2/28

TIME:	WHAT YOU ATE AND THE AMOUNT:	WHAT YOU DRANK:	WHERE WERE YOU?	WERE YOU HUNGRY? Y/N:
6:45 a.m.	Oatmeal made with ½ cup of skim milk, ½ grapefruit, almonds ½ cup of oatmeal, 6 ounces of skim milk, 13 almonds, ½ grapefruit	2 cups of coffee with ½ cup of 1% milk	Kitchen table	Y
10:30 a.m.	1 hard-cooked egg, 6 strawberries	8 ounces of water	Desk at work	Y

As you can see, this time around, we're asking you to pay attention not just to what you ate but how much you ate. After measuring your portion sizes in Chapter 5, this shouldn't be hard to do. Now you know how much you're eating, right? Also, we're asking you to note whether or not you're hungry. In an ideal world, you'll finish

Serving Suggestion: Texture, Not Taste

Not everyone loves fresh chickpeas, kidney beans, or black beans—although sometimes that's because of texture not taste. Here's a serving suggestion for Crunchy Garbanzos (a.k.a. chickpeas) from Leslie.

Drain and rinse a can of chickpeas. Blot them dry with paper towels. Put them in a bowl, drizzle with 2 teaspoons of olive oil, and mix. Spread the chickpeas onto a baking sheet. Sprinkle with a little salt, pepper, garlic salt, or cayenne, if desired. Roast in a 400-degree oven until they're crunchy and brown, about 30 minutes, stirring once. A ½-cup serving packs 6 grams of protein. They can be added to salads or eaten alone—no fork necessary!

your log and have a column full of yeses. But if you have some nos in there too, at least you know those are places where you can cut some calories.

Here's something about those amounts: You can't write "handful" in there. Everyone has a different-size hand! Is it an overflowing handful or a little nibble? Get out your measuring cup and measure. When you make yourself do this, it takes a lot of the "mindless" out of eating. First, you're forced to ask yourself if you're really hungry. If you're not, it usually stops you in your tracks. And if you are, it keeps your portions in check.

LUNCHES TO LIFT YOU

While breakfast might be the most important meal of the day, lunch takes on special significance, especially during the workweek. Lunch has to revive you, fuel you, get you through your afternoon.

So here are some ways to amp up your midday meal:

- *Have* **a midday meal!** A couple of crackers or a Nutri-Grain bar is not sufficient. Yes, I know you're busy. We're all busy. Eat a decent lunch now, and you'll save time when you don't crash at 2 p.m. and scurry off for coffee and something from the vending machine. If you're taking care of yourself, at least 15 minutes for lunch should be nonnegotiable.

- **Power up the protein.** Aim to get one-third of your daily allotment at lunch. Instead of ordering a big, bready sandwich with a bulky roll and one slice of deli turkey, try the opposite: A thinner bread, like pita or a wrap, and at least three slices of meat, which will get you about 10 grams of protein.

- **Think outside the sandwich.** Lunch doesn't have to exist only within two slices of bread. Bring leftovers from last night's dinner. Order an omelet if you eat out for lunch. Have a bowl of chili. Or a burrito.

- **Or spruce up the sandwich.** During high school, I packed myself a turkey sandwich every day so I wouldn't have to eat the school lunch. After I graduated and went to college, I didn't eat another turkey sandwich for 10 years. When I interviewed Leslie for this book, she shared with me all the ways to embellish a sandwich: honey mustard or Jack Daniel's mustard. Sierra turkey instead of plain old turkey. Spinach, sprouts, onions. A thin slice of Cheddar or a sprinkle of feta. Different breads: caraway rye on Monday, a wrap on Tuesday, a roll for Hump Day. Make your sandwich an art form; don't bore your tastebuds before your first bite. As fast-food chains go, Subway does an admirable job with the sandwich.

- **Beware the salad.** Many people who are "dieting" stick to salads for lunch. And while they take awhile to chew, they don't do a whole lot to fill you up unless you top them with substantial protein, like

3 ounces of tuna, $\frac{1}{2}$ cup of cottage cheese, a hard-cooked egg, beans, or tofu. At the same time, salads can attract a lot of items that run up the calorie total quickly, like dressings, cheese, croutons, nuts, and dried fruits. So if your go-to lunch is a salad, and you're stuck in a weight loss rut, you might want to relegate it to a side for now and try a different main course for lunch.

- **Eat two distinct items.** Make lunch taste like a real meal with at least one "side." Your best bet is to choose a fruit or a vegetable as the second item. If you're having a sandwich, make sure you're also having something else such as a pear, apple, grapefruit, two clementines, a side salad, a serving of last night's veggies, baby carrots, bell pepper sticks, or chunky tomato soup. Those veggies or fruits will contribute to satiety—in other words, you'll still feel full a few hours later.

- **Bottoms up.** Aim for 20 ounces of liquid. It doesn't all have to be water, but we don't mean martinis, either. A cup of soup is good for 8 ounces. A big mug of tea also counts toward your total. "People tend to neglect the fluid at lunchtime," Leslie says, "but you need it to help fill you up and keep the system functioning optimally."

If you're eating a solid lunch at noon, you shouldn't be ravenous again by 2. In an ideal world, you eat lunch and you're not hungry again until about 4 hours later. So get ready to do some detective work. How soon are you hungry after lunch? If it's within a couple of hours, how can you transform your lunchtime meal to tide you over longer?

The midday lull is another matter entirely. Many folks (yours truly included) find themselves noshing midafternoon, not out of hunger but out of fatigue or boredom. One strategy for combating this is to divide your lunch. Eat half a sandwich and half of your baby carrots at noon, then eat the other half at 2 p.m., when you'd otherwise be tempted to check out what Dunkin' has to offer.

HOLIDAY SURVIVAL GUIDE

Smack dab in the middle of the test panelists' walking and eating program, Thanksgiving hit. Seriously, right in Stage 5. Just when these determined folks were getting the hang of some of the principles of healthier eating, holiday temptation season rolled around.

The Sunday before Thanksgiving, Leslie sent out some tips about how to deal with the national stuff-yourself-silly day. The good thing is, these tips work for *any* holiday whether it's Easter dinner or a Fourth of July barbecue. The key is acknowledging that food is the main event at the day's celebration and realizing you have to be prepared to deal with it. Here are Leslie's lessons:

- **Plan a holiday morning walk.** A brisk jaunt can help reinforce healthy food choices later in the day because you don't want to undo the good-for-you steps you just took.

- **Eat breakfast as you normally would.** And if the main meal is being served later in the day, eat lunch as you normally would so you're not famished when you sit down to dinner. Get some protein, fruit, and vegetables in at breakfast and lunch.

- **Be careful of the nibbles before the dinner.** You want to avoid sitting down to a holiday meal being already stuffed.

- **Don't deprive yourself at dinner.** Let's be honest: The food is the centerpiece of Thanksgiving—and many other holidays, too. If you've been anticipating your sister-in-law's mushroom stuffing for 364 days, you should have some. Take a spoonful of everything you want to try. It doesn't have to be a heaping serving.

- **Eat slowly.** Savor every bite of the mushroom stuffing. Enjoy the flavors. Talk to your meal companions.

- **Utilize your utensils.** You can still use your small plate or small fork at Christmas, Easter, or the Memorial Day picnic. No one has to notice.

- **Save your calories for the foods that are really special and you really want to taste.** Don't bother with store-bought rolls or those little cheese cubes, which are available anytime.

- **Get up between the main course and dessert.** See if you can interest anyone in an easy walk—or, at the very least, load the dishwasher. Give your gut a break.

- **Have smaller pieces of pie for dessert.** And if you're making the pumpkin pie—which, incidentally, is the healthiest pie option—Leslie recommends using evaporated skim milk instead of cream and a gingersnap crust instead of a regular pie crust.

- **Bringing something? Go green.** Sugar snap peas. Salad. Roasted asparagus. "When you think about it, Thanksgiving dinner is kind of brown," Leslie says. "Turkey, stuffing, potato, pumpkin pie. Where's the color?" Her go-to Thanksgiving salad is baby spinach, mandarin oranges, and dried cranberries, with a little light dressing of orange and grapefruit juice whisked together with olive oil. "It looks beautiful, it tastes great, it brings color to the plate, and it's a nice complement to the other heavy foods that are there," she says. "And it's a lot easier than making the stuffing!"

- **Be forgiving as well as thanks-giving.** When it's over, acknowledge that you probably ate more on that one day than you wanted. But that doesn't mean the rest of the Thanksgiving weekend has to be a disaster. Sure, everyone "sins" on Thanksgiving. Fine, move on. But avoid the "I've blown it" mentality, which goes something like this: "Oh, I'm so bad. I'll never change, so I might as well keep eating leftovers and extra pie all weekend." That rationale results in behavior more damaging than just enjoying a big meal at Thanksgiving.

To-Do List

☐ Take a look at your calendar to plan at least five times you can walk during the next week.

☐ Complete at least five workouts, including at least 2 brisk walks, 2 speed walks, and your second challenge walk. Don't schedule speed walks and/or challenge walks on back-to-back days. Make a note of how far you go during your challenge walk.

☐ Complete at least 2 sets of strength exercises on nonconsecutive days.

☐ Figure out how many grams of protein you need, which is roughly one-half of your ideal body weight.

☐ Examine your lunch. Are you getting about one-third of your daily allotment of protein? Are you full after you eat lunch for several hours? If not, how can you fix the meal to stay satiated longer?

Age: 55

Height: 5'9"

Total pounds lost:
17.6 pounds
in 12 weeks

Total inches lost:
15½ inches,
**including 3 inches from
her waist and
3¾ inches from her hips**

Starting walk time:
17:35

Ending walk time:
14:27

Faster by:
3 minutes
8 seconds

Before

Gayle Hendricks

Day job: I'm a graphic designer, and I teach classes at two different colleges.

How I got here: I've been struggling with my weight since my twenties.

How I started: A few years back, I didn't have health insurance. I was at a health fair, and I had my blood pressure taken, and it was really high. They wanted to call an ambulance for me. I went to a doctor at one of those urgent care clinics. He gave me medication and suggested exercise.

I would sit on the couch and think of every excuse in the book not to walk. There's a cloud; it might rain. That's when I decided I needed a goal. When I saw a commercial on TV for the Komen 3-Day walk, I decided to train for it and do it. And when I got home from that, I started looking up 5-Ks I could walk. Otherwise, I would be back to making excuses for not going out.

Winning strategies:
I need a goal. If I don't have a goal, I get very complacent. I'll do 5-Ks, 10-Ks, ultra walks, even stairclimbs. When I walked 1:43:58 for a 10-K, I was really pleased. (That's a 16:30-minute mile, on average.)

Nutrition advice: I'm trying really hard to watch what I eat and take it easy on the carbs and the sugar. The week after the Walk Your Butt Off! program ended, I did backslide. I ate everything on my forbidden list. It seemed wonderful, but I found I didn't enjoy all those carbs and sugar as much as I did before.

Work in progress: I'm fighting not grazing. I still eat at times of stress.

CHAPTER 7

KEEPING Your Momentum

On three occasions, the folks on the Walk Your Butt Off! test panel took time off from work to come to Rodale headquarters.

At both the beginning and end of the 12-week session, everyone was photographed and tested for weight, measurements, and walking speed.

It was the 6-week midpoint check-in. However, it proved to be highly emotional.

I never expected that emotion when I arrived that morning at 7. First, we weighed everyone in and took their measurements. Then, after getting an official printout of their progress for the first 6 weeks of the program, panelists moved into an office in groups of two and three to talk to Leslie.

She spent 4 hours on speakerphone that morning, answering every question that came her way, from Christmas cookies and serving suggestions to strategies for combating the evening munchies and where to find edamame. I sat in the corner with my laptop, taking notes on what she told people.

Many were happy, and a few were elated. Most members of the panel had shed a few pounds already; some had lost double-digit amounts.

Then there were the ones who had lost less weight than they expected. In more than one case, I was glad Leslie was in Pittsburgh, safe from their wrath. One woman marched into the office and declared, "I have done everything you two have asked! Every workout, every eating tip. I'm walking around my neighborhood like a crazy lady! And I've lost only 3 pounds! Three little pounds!"

The final panelist that day, Bethany Lee, came up to be measured while her husband and 6-month-old infant waited in the lobby. She disappeared into the measurement room and came out a few minutes later, valiantly holding back tears. "The friend I walk with," she told us, "is dropping weight like crazy. And I'm exactly the same." At that point, her weight was the same as it had been 6 weeks earlier, to the tenth of a pound. She then went on to tell us about the health problems she had after her son's premature birth, which sent her back to the hospital as a patient while her son was in the NICU. Leslie responded that given the trauma her body had been through just a few months earlier, perhaps her body wasn't ready for weight loss just yet.

That evening, I sent a pep talk e-mail to the folks who had voiced their frustrations. Here it is:

Hi, everyone!

I wanted to follow up because I know there was a fair amount of frustration among some people on Thursday that the numbers on the scale aren't always reflecting the hard work you're putting in. There are lots of reasons for that—everything from the clothes you wore, time of day you were weighed, what you ate. Your scale weight can fluctuate about 5 pounds a day and even more throughout the month for women. We can't control some of these things.

Michele, Leslie, and I all know this and would never be mad at you or disappointed in you if you don't see a change in the number on the scale or a change of the magnitude you were expecting. We're pulling for you, and we want you to get the results you want. If you're disappointed, we feel badly, too.

Your dedication to the program and doing your best to stick with the workouts are what is important—and it's showing. Almost everyone mentioned feeling more energetic; no one told me they were more lethargic. In a few cases where weight increased, body fat decreased. Blood pressures fell. Inches melted away from waistlines. Please remember: The scale is only one, imperfect measure of health. After nearly 7 weeks, the complete picture looks better for everyone. Forget about the scale and focus on the positive benefits that you're seeing in other areas.

The other important point to note is that every body is different. Some people lose faster in the beginning and then plateau, while others take longer to get started but then see dramatic changes—even when everyone is following the same program. So, don't give up—big changes might be right around the corner.

Finally, Walk Your Butt Off! is an experiment. This program hasn't been tried before in this way. Your feedback—the good and the bad—will help us learn what works and what doesn't. And your experience is going to help inspire and motivate thousands of others.

Thanks again for your dedication. You've come this far. Don't give up! And we're here to help you, so let us know if there's anything we can do.

Sarah

IGNORE THE SCALE

We weren't kidding about anything in that e-mail. We weren't try-ing to brush aside their concerns but to point out what we know to be true: Different bodies respond to exercise in different ways. Peo-ple respond to changes in their food intake differently, too. Some start losing weight immediately. For others, it takes awhile to get the rock rolling down the hill, and only once it gets rolling does it pick up speed.

The scale spits out an instantaneous response every time you step on it, so it's hard to ignore. And if you weigh yourself frequently and find your weight going up, you can check yourself before it gets out of hand. But the scale is just one data point.

Other measures of health might be harder to pinpoint, but they're equally deserving of your attention: the energy in your days, the quality of your sleep, the way your pants fit, the way you feel after you run to catch a bus or a toddler. One test panelist, Sandra Hamill, mentioned that she thought her skin looked brighter. All these things tell you a great deal—probably more—about your total physical condition than that device you keep in your bathroom.

With walking, it takes awhile to build up momentum. The more you walk, the easier it is to walk. And when it's easier to walk, you walk more. Success begets success.

If you feel you're not making enough progress, I urge you to keep going for another week. Also, think about where you *are* seeing improvements. If the scale says you're the same weight but your workdays are more productive because of your newfound energy, doesn't that count for something? You're more than halfway through the program, and if you haven't noticed improvements in your health and ability already, you will soon. Keep at it.

WALK YOUR BUTT OFF!

STAGE 7

Minimum: 5 walks
Strength workouts*: 2–3 times this week

2 TO 4 BRISK WALKS

After warming up by walking at an easy pace for 2 to 3 minutes, you should walk at a purposeful pace, as if you need to get to an appointment, about 3 to 4 mph, for 30 to 40 minutes. Do a minimum of 2 brisk walks this week; a maximum of 4 if you're trying to walk every day.

Total workout time: 32–43 minutes

2 SPEED WALKS

➤ Start with a 2-minute warm-up at an easy pace.

➤ Then do 1 minute at a brisk pace and 4 minutes at a fast pace 4 times.

➤ End with 3 minutes of easy walking.

Total fast walking time: 16 minutes.
Total workout time: 25 minutes.

1 CHALLENGE WALK

➤ Start with a 5-minute warm-up (2 minutes easy, 3 minutes brisk).

➤ Then do 10 minutes as fast as you can, noting your starting point and finishing point or distance.

➤ Return and walk back to the start at a more comfortable pace.

Total workout time: At least 25 minutes

*For the strength workout, see page 75.

ON THE BACK NINE

When you completed Stage 6, you made it halfway through the Walk Your Butt Off! program. Congratulations! You've done at least 30 walks at this point—likely more if you're walking more than 5 days per week or if you've spent an extra week or two on a particular stage. Hopefully, your log book is filling up with notes about these efforts. Flip back through the pages to check out all the writing. It starts to look like an impressive body of work, right?

With this week's workouts, we're up to 16 minutes of fast walking per week. (Remember the Stage 1 workout? It was only 4 minutes.)

Because you're pushing the pace in longer and longer segments, it's helpful if you can devote a few minutes of attention to your form during every workout. Maybe on a speed walk day, you spend one fast walking segment focusing on a different part of your body: the arms, the gaze, the foot strike, the way you push off. Below is this week's tip to help with your arms.

TECHNIQUE TIP #6

• Swing your arms

This week, let's add some power to your arm swing by recruiting your back muscles. This will also help to tone your back. Imagine that your back muscles are pulling your arms back. Squeeze your shoulder blades and drive your elbows behind you, keeping them close to your body (not swinging out to the sides). Then let one arm swing naturally forward as you pull the other one back so the work is on the back swing. Remember to keep your shoulders down and relaxed, not pulled up toward your ears. Practice in a mirror while standing still to get the hang of it. It's also a great warm-up before you do a strength workout.

CONTINUE CROSS-TRAINING

The athletic résumés of our test panelists varied widely. Some were true couch potatoes; others had played college sports. Several had hiked in the mountains, and one had done a 3-day endurance walk for breast cancer research. Others? Not much more than walking their dogs.

If you have time, it's great if you can keep up any activities you were doing before you started the Walk Your Butt Off! routine. Panelist Charlene Nelson stuck with Zumba, which she enjoyed with her friends. Lorraine Wiedorn stayed devoted to her Pilates tape, especially when it was too wet to walk outside. Val Donohue, a college basketball coach, uses the same weight room her players do to keep up her muscle tone. And Gayle Hendricks continues signing up for road races, which she walks because she enjoys getting out with a group of people, wearing a number, and having a clock and a finish line. Those "racewalks" helped her stay active and motivated.

Any bit of activity you do in a day will help your fitness and will help you burn calories. And you will probably find that regular walking improves your abilities in other sports, whether it's tennis, Zumba, or swimming.

ALL-WEATHER WALKING

For avid outdoor walkers, investing in a few key pieces of clothing will improve your chances of exercising even when it's windy, rainy, icy, or snowy. On cold days, layers are the way to go. "Start with a base layer made of a wicking fabric, which keeps sweat away from your skin and keeps you dry. CoolMax or polypropylene are two examples," Coach Michele says. "The next layer is insulation, like a fleece fabric such as Polartec. And top it off with a wind- and waterproof jacket with zipped vents you can open and close as you warm up and cool down. Of course, don't forget a hat and gloves. For ice, I recommend slip-on cleats like Yaktrax or Stabilicers. Check Dick's, Sports Authority, L.L. Bean, or REI for them. Year-round walking can actually be very enjoyable with the right gear."

FOOD TALK:
HIDDEN SABOTEURS

We hereby invite you to look at the food log you just completed. Sit down with it for a few minutes when you won't be interrupted. Read it.

Keeping a food log alone won't help you eat better. You have to look at what the log shows, understand how you're eating, and then make changes accordingly. No point in keeping a log and then shoving it in a drawer.

Using your log as a guide, this is a good time to do a calorie tally to get a sense of what you're consuming in a day. It's not something you need to think about too much if the idea of putting numbers on your food drives you nuts. All the same, it's good to have a ballpark idea of how many calories you're eating. Simple smartphone apps such as MyPlate and Web sites like CalorieKing.com and the Food-A-Pedia directory at www.choosemyplate.gov/SuperTracker can give you a good idea.

So, how's it going? Remember when you answered the question back in Chapters 1 and 3 about what your biggest eating challenge is? How are you doing on that? Are you better off, worse off, or about the same? Are there any meals or times during the day that are higher calorically than you expected?

We'll give you a few lines on the following page to write in some updates about your progress on your initial area of concern. Or, turn to page 265 in the workbook section for more room.

Is that eating habit still a problem for you? If you've made the changes you wanted to make and they seem to be sticking, what's next on your eating agenda?

_____

_____

_____

SUCCESSFUL SNACKING

For a long time, conventional wisdom has been that in order to lose weight, you need to eat six small meals per day rather than three large ones. With six small meals, the thinking goes, you never get too hungry and you won't overeat when you do sit down to eat.

I asked Leslie about that. She thinks it's bunk.

The only part of the six-small-meals rationale that she endorses is not overeating at any one meal. But this constant eating thing? Grazing? No good. It's bad for your teeth, it's bad for your digestive system, and it obscures you from having any awareness of when you're hungry and when you're full. America is the only country in the world that eats this way.

Which isn't to say you shouldn't ever have a snack. If you eat three meals and two small snacks, fine. Just be careful of how you define "snack." A snack should be premeditated. A snack is an eating occasion, served from a plate, when you pay attention to the food going into your mouth and actually taste it. A snack is not license to put your hand in a bag of pretzels and stuff a bunch in your mouth every few minutes until the bag is half gone.

If you've been reading closely up until now, you can probably predict what Leslie thinks make good snack choices. Here are some parameters:

- If you're hungry and you need something to tide you over until the next meal, have a snack. Make it substantial enough—200 to 250 calories—so that you feel satisfied and so the snack serves its purpose: It gets you to the next meal without wanting to eat the legs off the nearest chair. If you try to stick to 100-calorie snacks, you'll likely be hungry again within 30 minutes or so. What's the point of that?

- Make your snack mimic a small meal. It should include protein, fiber, and carbohydrate. Put it on a small plate or a saucer.

- A satisfying snack will include two items or more. Instead of just a piece of string cheese, make it string cheese, a couple of whole wheat crackers, and an apple. Half of a turkey sandwich. A bowl of cereal with milk. A mini pita with carrots and hummus. V8 juice or tomato juice (yep, they're vegetables) to go along with your pretzels.

- If you rely on bars for snacks, read the labels carefully. Make sure the bar has at least 5 grams of protein and comes in around 200 calories. A lot of bars have more calories than that and some are primarily carbohydrate, so keep your eyes open. If you choose a smaller bar, say, one that's about 150 calories, you can have your second item, like a piece of fruit, to go with it.

THE HEALTH HALO

I recently steered my cart down the aisle of the supermarket and saw a freestanding display of WhoNu? cookies. I picked up a box and read the label for the chewy chocolate chip variety. In three cookies: 150 calories, 11 grams of sugar, 2 grams of protein, 3 grams of fiber. *Well, not bad,* I thought to myself. Sure beats Nestlé Tollhouse Chocolate Chip Cookies (just *one* cookie made from a tub of dough has 130 calories and 11 grams of sugar).

Later that night, I was e-mailing with Leslie and told her about my "find." Her response was swift: "A cookie is still a cookie," she told me.

She went on to explain: Whether a cookie has butter, shortening, olive oil, sugar, molasses, or agave, it doesn't matter because one of anything is not the issue. Eat the whole box of cookies or an entire sleeve, and there's a problem. And sometimes, Leslie says, one "real" chocolate chip cookie can be more satisfying than the "healthier" cookie. What's cooked up in a laboratory somewhere to be supposedly good for you doesn't always taste the best. The small portion of the real thing will satisfy your sweet tooth better than several of the low-fat, low-sugar, or, in this case, high-fiber imitations, so in the end you'll consume fewer calories by eating the true cookie.

This is what Leslie and other experts refer to as the "health halo." Foods that are labeled "fat free," "organic," "diet," or even "natural" often lull us into thinking we can eat several serving sizes without a problem. That's simply not true.

Organic potato chips are still potato chips. Something might be labeled "sugar free," but chances are, it's not calorie free. "Reduced-fat" peanut butter, for instance, has exactly the same number of calories as regular peanut butter. A product's packaging might make a food look healthy, but you still have to read the nutrition facts to get the real deal.

And those "diet" foods often leave you rooting around in your cabinets for something to nosh on later. Ask yourself: Does this snack really do it for me, or am I hungry a half hour after I finish it? "The label might scream 'health food,' but if it's not satisfying, it's probably not worth the extra money you pay for foods like that," Leslie says.

SCRUTINIZE YOUR SALAD

Salad is another food that wears a health halo. The lettuce and veggies are fine. No problems there.

But when a line chef in a restaurant kitchen adds croutons, nuts, and blue cheese crumbles and douses it with ½ cup of dressing, you can have a calorie bomb. Ask for dressing on the side, put it on yourself, and be aware of the high-fat, high-calorie add-ins.

STAT SHEET

Charlene Nelson

Age: 50

Total pounds lost:
5.2 pounds
in 12 weeks

Total inches lost:
5¾ inches,
including 1¾ inches
from her waist and
2 inches from her hips

Walk time: Faster by
1 minute
34 seconds

Big wins: Keeping a food log helped me see all I was eating *while* I was cooking dinner for my son. I hate to waste food, so when he was done, I would eat whatever was left on his plate. That's not necessary. So I focused on my mindless eating, the ghost eating. When you have to write it down, it kind of guilts you into not eating that handful of cheese. I made myself eat at the table. You can eat a whole meal when you're cooking.

Next steps: The more you work out, when you're on a roll, you crave it. I sometimes felt like the workouts weren't long enough. It took me at least 5 minutes to get all warmed up. I think I can do more.

And if you think you're "being good" by eating just a salad at lunch, beware that the strategy doesn't backfire later, when you're so hungry in the afternoon that you indulge in the nearest pastry. That's why we recommend having a lean protein with the salad, such as chicken, tuna, tofu, or a hard-cooked egg.

JAVA JUNK

Coffee and tea can be problematic, too. This issue came up with many of our test panelists in their discussions with Leslie. Coffee and tea have basically zero calories. Start adding creamer and sugar, and you can easily run a drink to 150 calories or more. Have two or three drinks like that a day, and it can explain why the numbers on the scale aren't changing.

I know it's not easy to mess with your coffee habits. I'm as addicted as anyone. Leslie recommends super skim milk to make coffee creamier. And measure the sugar; don't just pour it from the spout of the sugar dispenser. Little by little, try to get used to less.

CHAPTER 7 ▸ To-Do List

☐ Take a look at your calendar to plan at least five times you can walk during the next week.

☐ Complete at least five workouts, including at least 2 brisk walks, 2 speed walks, and your third challenge walk. Don't schedule speed walks and/or challenge walks on back-to-back days. Make a note of how far you go during your challenge walk.

☐ Complete at least 2 sets of strength exercises on nonconsecutive days.

☐ Spend a few minutes thinking about the walking you've been doing and what you've noticed. Are you faster? Are you sleeping more soundly? Do you have more energy during the day?

☐ Analyze your food log to assess your snack choices. Are you getting more calories from snacks than you should? How can you change your snacks to make them include protein, fiber, and carbohydrate—and make sure they're satisfying?

Age: **52**

Height: **5'5"**

Total pounds lost:
7.6 pounds
in 12 weeks

Total inches lost:
8½ inches,
including 3¾ inches
from her waist and
2¼ inches from her hips

Starting walk time:
19:14

Ending walk time:
13:25

Faster by:
**5 minutes
49 seconds**

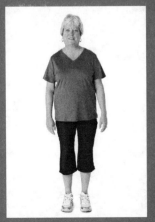

Before

Sandra Hamill

Day job: I work in sales support for a medical equipment manufacturer, and I'm married, with two grown sons.

How I got here: My job is a desk job. The lack of movement really affected me, and my weight gradually went up.

How I started: I mostly walked in the morning before work. If I did it in the morning, it got done.

Winning strategies: I listen to my music—country, Tim McGraw, some Christian gospel. I love to hear the song "These Boots Are Made for Walkin'" when I'm working out.

Nutrition pointers: Portion control was the biggest factor for me. You don't need 8 ounces of steak. Leslie suggested I try the smaller plates and smallest size spoon and fork. By the last 2 weeks, I did not feel hungry at all.

Workout motivation: I walk on the rail trail near my house, and each time, I would try to walk a little farther, counting the houses that back up against it, just one house more. Sometimes during the workday, I'll do a lap around the campus of the office. It takes about 20 minutes.

Side effects: These days, I hit the pillow and I'm out. I used to wake up at 2 a.m. and roam—I'd unload the dishwasher and have a cup of tea. Now my sleep is so much better, and I have energy in the afternoon. And my skin seems so much brighter.

Best advice: Diet and exercise need to go hand in hand. The more you move, the more you pay attention to what is going into your body. You start to make that connection. I tell people to just start moving. You can walk half a mile.

CHAPTER 8

It Pays
TO BE
Restless

If fidgeting were an Olympic sport, Coach Michele would win a gold medal.

She has trouble standing still to brush her teeth. She often does a few squats every night in front of the bathroom mirror while she's cleaning those pearly whites. I can just picture it: squat, spit, squat, spit. When she was working at *Prevention*, she rarely made an interoffice phone call. Why should she when she could walk down the hall and see the person she was looking for?

Leslie is constantly moving, too. She gives dozens of speeches each year, and onstage, she's always pacing. Videographers the world over get nauseous trying to keep the camera trained on her as she walks back and forth, back and forth.

Me, I just enjoy picking up the pace whenever possible. Have you ever racewalked through a grocery store? It's kind of fun. I usually save this for off-peak times when I don't need a cart and I'm going in just because we're out of milk. Can't do this with the kids. Anyway, you go in, you're on a mission, and you've got your arms bent as if you're doing a speed walk, zooming toward the dairy case. I find myself counting steps as I go down the aisle. Whoosh, grab the milk, speed walk back to the cashier, speed walk to the car, and out of there. Yes, people look at me a little funny. So what?

I have trouble sitting for long periods of time, especially in front of the TV. I just get restless, I guess. So during commercial breaks, I'll stretch, do some leg swings, or try to hold a plank. Makes me feel better.

NO-SWEAT EXERCISING

Scientists have a name for this: NEAT, which stands for nonexercise activity thermogenesis. It's defined by researchers at the Mayo Clinic as the energy expended for everything we do that is not sleeping, eating, or sportslike exercise. So maybe Michele's nighttime squats and my commercial break planks are sportslike exercise and don't really count as NEAT.

But what researchers have found over time is this: The more you move during a day, the easier it is to stay lean. All those small ways we move over the course of a 24-hour period help burn calories. It's not only the 30 minutes per day of focused exercise time that matter; the other movements you make help keep you thin, too. Stay still, and you're more likely to hold on to your fat.

Another name for this is SPA: spontaneous physical activity, which is low-intensity physical activity. It's standing up to cook a meal, walking outside to get the mail, stretching at your desk, standing up for a phone call, or walking around a room while you're on the phone. These things aren't going to make you sweat or breathe hard. But boost the level of activity—any activity—in your day, and you're better off.

Scientists still argue about the causes of the obesity epidemic in America. Dr. Steven Blair, of the University of South Carolina, thinks our lack of movement is to blame: "I think the major cause is declining occupational energy expenditure and declining energy expenditure in the home," he says. "Take microwave ovens. I can remember when there was no such thing as frozen food. You had to buy it and wash it and slice it and chop it and stir it. And that takes more energy."

Yes, standing while chopping an onion burns a few calories. Not a lot but certainly more than pressing a few numbers on a microwave.

Human beings weren't built for long days in the car, hours in front of a computer, or evenings in front of a TV. People who live like that are prone to "sitting disease," which includes a range of problems such as obesity, cardiovascular disease, and type 2 diabetes.

In 2012, researchers at the University of Missouri published a study that showed how when people who were normally active cut down on their activity, their blood sugar levels spiked after meals.

Humans are meant to move.

WHAT CAN YOU DO?

In two words: Move more.

If you're getting your workouts in, great. That's a positive development, and for many people, five workouts a week is a huge lifestyle change. But know this: You can maximize your weight loss results and your health if you keep moving, even when the workout is over. A few extra steps each day, a few extra minutes on your feet—it all counts toward the calorie burn that will power your weight loss.

Dr. Blair is a prime example of this. He exercises first thing in the morning, usually a walk or a jog or some combination of the two. The rest of the day, he finds ways to move. Even though his seniority grants him the privilege to park in any lot on the University of South Carolina campus, he picks a spot that's 800 steps away, so that adds 1,600 steps to his daily total. He's a guy who confesses to using a bathroom in a different building from his office just to get up and walk more.

Dr. Blair has a lofty goal for himself: 5 million steps a year. That works out to 13,698 steps a day. That's a lot of activity. We'll get into pedometers more in the next chapter, but for now, just know this: There's a 72-year-old guy in South Carolina who is walking 5 million steps a year. So don't you think you might take the stairs just once in a while?

I pressed Dr. Blair a little about his lifestyle: Are there sacrifices you make to get those extra steps in? What about the time it takes?

I'm always in a hurry, I reasoned with him. I might have the best intentions to leave the house early to take a longer walk into an office, but when I'm constantly running late, I'd be tempted to park close by. He brushed me off. "I'm busy, too, working 70 hours per week," he says. "I watch only 1 hour of TV on most days. Americans on average watch 4 to 5 hours of TV, but they claim they are too busy to take three 10-minute walks."

Okay, then is walking in the morning enough? If you do your 30 minutes and sit in front of a computer all day, does that 30 minutes give you a free pass on activity for the rest of the day? "We don't really have the firm answer on that yet," Dr. Blair says. "I suspect you get additional [health] benefits if you don't sit quite so much. Again, let's come to the feeling. You're a writer, you've been sitting for 2 hours, and you get up and move around. Don't you feel better? Don't you think you can concentrate better when you sit back down?"

Can't argue with that. Remember these principles: With 30 minutes of moderate exercise every day, no matter what your weight, you'll be healthier than someone who is thin and sedentary. But if it's weight loss you're after, then the more you move, the more calories you'll burn and the easier it will be to lose. And the more weight you lose, the easier it becomes to move, so you'll move more. It becomes a reinforcing circle of good behavior.

What are some ways to move more?

- Use commercial breaks for walking in place, jumping jacks, or body weight exercises.

- Park as soon as you can in any parking lot, no matter how far you are from the store. You'll save gas, too.

- Avoid drive-thrus. Go inside to see the bank teller, the librarian, or the pharmacist. You're better off skipping the fast food, but if you're going to eat it, at least spend the time and calories to walk inside and stand in line.

STAGE 8

Minimum: 5 walks
Strength workouts*: 2–3 times this week

2 TO 4 BRISK WALKS

After warming up by walking at an easy pace for 2 to 3 minutes, you should walk at a purposeful pace, as if you need to get to an appointment, about 3 to 4 mph, for 30 to 40 minutes. Do a minimum of 2 brisk walks this week; a maximum of 4 if you're trying to walk every day.

Total workout time: 32–43 minutes

2 SPEED WALKS

➤ Start with a 2-minute warm-up at an easy pace.

➤ Then do 1 minute at a brisk pace and 6 minutes at a fast pace 3 times.

➤ End with 3 minutes of easy walking.

Total fast walking time: 18 minutes.
Total workout time: 26 minutes.

1 CHALLENGE WALK

➤ Start with a 5-minute warm-up (2 minutes easy, 3 minutes brisk).

➤ Then do 10 minutes as fast as you can, noting your starting point and finishing point or distance.

➤ Return and walk back to the start at a more comfortable pace.

Total workout time: At least 25 minutes

For the strength workout, see page 75.

- Be aggressive about folding laundry. Fold two shirts and walk to the room to put them away. Don't fold in front of the TV if it means you'll wait until the commercial break—when you have a towering pile—to put it all away.

- Stand up to prepare a meal now and then. Stay on your feet for an hour at a time.

- Stand up for 15 minutes on the hour at work. Move your computer so you can work on it while standing; adjustable desks are good for this. Stand up for phone calls. Invite your colleagues for walking meetings.

- Walk your dog or borrow a canine friend from a shelter for walks, which benefits you, the pooch, and the shelter. Veterinarians say that canine obesity rates are soaring, too.

- Walk some laps around the field or the parking lot while your kids are at soccer practice or in the swimming pool. Honestly, you're not a bad parent if you don't see every second of their *practices*.

These are things you can do that don't require extra time. You can do them during the course of your day just by making some adjustments to your routine.

That said, you have to keep up the regular activity you've worked so hard to establish. Stage 8 takes you to the next level. Here's a convenient advantage of pushing your speed segments to 6 minutes: You don't have to check your watch so often!

Remember, you can repeat any stage as many times as you want. So if you felt like Stage 7, with 4-minute speed walks, was a challenge, spend another week there before attempting Stage 8. There's no harm in that. Or you can opt for a "bridge" week, where you do intervals of 1 minute brisk/5 minutes fast to get you up to the Stage 8 level. Another idea is to be creative with the workouts and try a ladder: 1 minute brisk, 4 minutes fast, then 1 minute brisk, 5 minutes fast, then 1 minute brisk, 6 minutes fast. Get it? While it's great if you can do the workouts exactly as they're laid out here, adapting them to your own needs is a smart alternative that may help improve your results.

The ultimate goal is to build to 25 minutes of continuous fast walking, but there's no deadline for that. If it takes you 13 or 14 or 18 weeks to get there, great. There's no rush.

And remember, keep an eye on that challenge walk. This is the best measure of how your speed is improving. Make a note of your progress in your log.

This is subtle. It's hard to feel a 5-degree lean. And it's a Technique Tip that's most important for people who are leaning back when they walk. So ask a friend to watch you and tell you if you're making this common walking mistake. If you are, try the slight shift forward from the ankles.

TECHNIQUE TIP # 7

Take advantage of gravity

Walking is actually a series of forward falls, and we catch ourselves with our front leg. But a common walking mistake is leaning back so you're resisting gravity. Instead, lean into your walk just a little bit—about 5 degrees—and the lean should come from your ankles. Don't bend at your waist. To get a feel for this, try it while standing still. You can do this by standing comfortably with your back and head lined up against a wall. Lean forward from the ankles, peeling your body off the wall just to the point when you feel your heels want to lift. Then carry that feeling over while you are walking. Just remember to keep your head up and look 10 to 20 feet in front of you.

GIVE CREDIT WHERE IT'S DUE

Coach Michele reminds you to toot your own horn. "Be kind to yourself," she says. "It's amazing how hard we can be on ourselves when we miss a workout." Research has shown that a key factor in sticking to exercise is the belief and confidence in your ability to do it. Negative thinking or self-talk seriously chips away at that confidence, making it harder to stick to your routine. The next time you miss a workout or are thinking about skipping one, pretend that you are your best friend. What would you say to her if she were struggling? Use that same supportive language to help yourself. Avoid negative "I can't" thoughts or other put-downs.

You might think positive affirmations are kind of hokey, but try them and see. Yes, this takes some practice, but try repeating these mantras before a workout or during the fast portions of a speed walk or challenge walk:

- I can do this.
- Look how well I did yesterday.
- I am getting stronger.

Anytime you notice toxic thoughts creeping in, think or say aloud "Stop!"

FOOD TALK:
LIQUID AND UNEXPECTED CHALLENGES

When you're exercising regularly, it's more important than ever to keep track of your fluid intake so you avoid dehydration. Arlene Scott from our test panel put a gallon of spring water on her kitchen counter. "It provided a visual reminder to drink, drink, drink," she says. "I find these fluids keep me satisfied." Arlene mostly drank tap water (the spring water was just a cue) and she used Crystal Light to flavor it on occasion. She also stocked her car with bottles so she could be more deliberate about her intake.

Women need 90 ounces (that's more than 11 cups) of liquid in a day; guys need more like 125 (close to 16 cups). That doesn't have to be all water, though! Coffee, tea, the milk you put on your cereal, soup—they all count. Also, liquid exists in fruits and vegetables. So if you're getting 4 to 5 servings daily of fruits and vegetables, you really only need to aim for about 70 ounces of liquid (women) and 100 (men). Anything *except* alcohol counts. Caffeinated beverages still contribute to your total.

"It's a myth that caffeine dehydrates you," Leslie says. "People think that coffee and tea make them produce more urine, but that's not true. Caffeine might increase your *urge* to go, but it's not as if you have to drink an additional cup of water for every cup of coffee in order to get the required liquid, or else you truly will be running to the bath-room every hour."

Why do you need so much of the wet stuff? For hydration. When you're walking, even if it's cold outside, you're still sweating and you need to replace what you sweat. Second, those ounces are what your body needs for its many different systems to function properly. Water helps you digest your food, for instance, and keeps your joints lubricated, which is important for exercisers. And liquid takes up more volume in your stomach. If you drink plenty with your meals, you'll feel fuller longer.

If you're not in the habit already, work on keeping a water bottle with you at your desk and in your car, and take a few extra swigs throughout the day. Like everything else, try adding small amounts at a time. You don't have to make a huge change all at once.

TROUBLESHOOTING YOUR DIET

When our test panelists checked in with Leslie midway through the program, they reported on what was going well and where they were

Jacqueline Macaione

The problem: Talk about a challenging environment for weight loss: Jacqueline, 49, is a taste tester at M&M Mars in New Jersey. Chocolate is her job.

Her big struggle with the WYBO! plan is the speed walks—especially timing the brisk and fast paces. "I used my iPhone to keep the time, but I got too easily distracted to pay attention after the third or fourth change and regularly lost track," she says.

Michele's solution: If keeping time is too much of a chore for her, she can use physical landmarks to break up the segments—count telephone poles or driveways, for instance—or simply go by feel. Going forward, she doesn't have to be a slave to the numbers as long as she gradually increases the amount of intensity during her speed days. Jacqueline expressed an interest in trying running, so if she wants to jog during her fast walking segments to raise the intensity, that's fine.

The analysis: Jacqueline walks with her dogs daily, making her a poster child for the power of NEAT. The walking has kept her weight in check over the years and helped keep her healthy. At 160 pounds and 5 foot 6 inches, she's not obese, and her blood pressure is at a healthy level: 100/90. Even with her complaints about the speed intervals, she was able to cut her mile walk time by 47 seconds, from 15:15 to 14:28.

Her take: You have to be ready mentally, and I finally was. When you're ready, then the excuses go away.

struggling. Remember, our group met during the holidays, so many of these challenging situations had to do with holiday celebrations. But challenges arise at any time of the year. The feedback was valuable, and their stories were so understandable that I distributed them to the group so everyone could learn from each other. Here are some of their tips:

Be honest and ask for support: Many folks had stories of how their nearest and dearest sabotaged their diets, either intentionally or inadvertently. For some people, food equals love, and sweets and rich foods are a sign of affection.

Kristen Tomasic told how over Thanksgiving, she had to travel to her in-laws. Her mother-in-law is a fabulous Italian cook, always trying to get everyone to eat more. So before the trip, Kristen called her mother-in-law and said, "Look, you know I love your cooking. But I'm on this program, and I'm trying to stick to it, and I'm still going to eat, but I'm not going to eat as much as usual. And I could really use your support with this." Her mother-in-law was understanding about it and very supportive.

Leslie's take: This was really smart. By bringing the issue into the open, she had the discussion one time and got her mother-in-law's agreement. Then Kristen didn't have to spend the rest of the week fending off attempts to feed her more than she wanted. The support and buy-in of relatives is crucial to success.

Nighttime noshing: Eating at night isn't bad—if you're hungry. Calories consumed at night don't store any differently than calories consumed during the day. But if you're eating out of boredom not hunger, then, yes, nighttime eating is a problem. Many test panelists said they struggled to control their intake at night.

Leslie's take: Remove yourself physically from the eating environment. If you tend to mindlessly eat when you're near the kitchen or in front of the TV, go to your bedroom and read. Or just sit or do something else for a while. Go for an extra 15-minute walk when the urges hit. Taking a moment to yourself, away from the kitchen, helps you gain control of the evening.

Second, identify a list of nighttime snacks that you like and find satisfying. Put the list on the inside of one of your kitchen cabinets. This list gives you a game plan for the evening. And whatever it is you

Age: 31

Height: 5'6"

Total pounds lost:
6.8 pounds
in 12 weeks

Total inches lost:
½ inch,
including 2 inches from
her hips and chest
but gaining 1½ inches
in her biceps

Starting walk time:
17:02

Ending walk time:
13:42

Faster by:
**3 minutes
20 seconds**

Before

Bethany Lee

Day job: I'm a babysitter and a stay-at-home mom, married with an infant.

How I got here: I have always struggled with my weight. I trained for the 3-day breast cancer walk and ended up in great shape. Then I met my husband, and things went south while we were dating. For the wedding, I lost a bit, then things went bad when I got pregnant.

How I started: After the birth of my son, I had some complications and ended up back in the hospital with an infection. When I was finally cleared to exercise, I was on a mission. I was so disappointed at the midpoint when my weight was exactly the same, but Leslie told me to be patient, and she reminded me that my body had just been through a trauma. The almost 7 pounds I lost was during the second half of the program.

Winning strategies: I loved that for most of the walks, I could bring my son in the stroller. I also got my neighbor into walking with me.

Nutrition pointers: Taking a bite here and there really adds to the calories. It really helped me to stop that and be more conscious of my snacking. I'm not eating meat anymore, so I have become very aware of getting enough protein and trying different sources.

Weather beaters: Once I am dressed to walk, I go no matter what. My neighbor and I walked one evening in a sleet storm. It was dark, and it was really coming down. My husband called to make sure we were okay. We were having so much fun, we actually added more time and distance!

Best advice: It is a lot easier to have a friend or a loved one beside you. You have to have it in your mind that you are ready to take the steps to better yourself. If you are not committed, then you will not each your goals.

decide you want at night, put it in a bowl, in a glass, or on a plate. That way, there's a limit to what you eat and you're not haphazardly grabbing for things.

Sometimes foods taste better in our memories than in our mouths: Steve Cobb said he had greatly improved his eating patterns during the first 7 weeks of the program, but he did have an occasional "binge." One evening, after downing several Danish butter cookies in quick succession, he actually felt sick from the taste and the amount, even though he had similar binges frequently in his past.

Leslie's take: Steve's experience is common. We often look forward to certain foods with a high degree of anticipation, and then we realize that we don't like how we feel physically after we've eaten them. So use that realization to help give you control when you're tempted. Tune in to those "aha!" moments.

Seven pounds of Godiva chocolate: Donna Karoly walked into her office one morning just before Christmas and faced gifts of chocolate from various business contacts totaling 7 pounds. So she ate one piece of dark chocolate and brought the rest downstairs to a different group of workers who don't normally get recognized during the holidays.

Leslie's take: That's a great example of changing the eating environment. Many people think they can stare at 7 pounds of chocolate and not touch it; others realize they have to get it out of their sight. You can't control what people bring to you, but you can control what stays near you.

To-Do List

☐ Take a look at your calendar to plan at least five times you can walk during the next week.

☐ Complete at least five workouts, including at least 2 brisk walks, 2 speed walks, and your fourth challenge walk. Don't schedule speed walks and/or challenge walks on back-to-back days. Make a note of how far you go during your challenge walk.

☐ Complete at least two sets of strength exercises on nonconsecutive days.

☐ Think about three ways you can add more movement into your day, whether at work or at home.

☐ Give yourself at least one compliment about your walking. Write it down.

☐ Check your fluid intake to make sure you're getting enough during the day. Women need at least **90** ounces; men need **125**.

CHAPTER 9

START
Counting
Steps

I ordered a pedometer on Amazon. I picked the Omron HJ-112, which had a middle-of-the-road price ($22.49) and looked easy to use.

(The prevailing wisdom is that any pedometer about $10 or more will be accurate enough. Pay less than that and the accuracy is probably compromised.) The thing hooks on your waistband or goes in your pocket. When it arrived, all I had to do was figure out my average stride length to program it, and the booklet made that plenty easy.

So the rule of thumb set forth by countless fitness experts is that walking 10,000 steps a day gives a person a healthy level of activity. That gets you up and moving and burns a fair amount of calories, assuming you aren't eating while you're walking.

Getting in 10,000 steps a day requires some planning unless you work in a job that has you on your feet all day long. It works out to roughly 5 miles per day of walking depending, of course, on how long a person's stride is. Test panelist Kristen Tomasic, who is something of a gear geek, tested this out for me. She covered about 5,800 steps in a 40-minute brisk walk. She did 143 steps per minute and averaged a pace slightly slower than 14 minutes per mile.

I'm with her. I can see that I get in about 6,300 steps in a 3-mile walking workout.

But the rest of the day, I sit pretty still. Stiller than I should be, as I hunch over my computer and write. I get a couple thousand steps in around the house, cooking, getting the mail, and folding laundry, but to hit 10,000, I need to take a second walk with my kids or do some laps around the yard. I have to think about how I'm going to do it if I really want to hit 10,000 steps.

The pedometer is a pretty good kick in the pants.

Like Kristen, I've become fascinated by the numbers. I realized that my morning routine—making the bed, getting showered and dressed, sitting down with some cereal—contributes almost nothing to the total. (For the record, I don't bring the pedometer into the shower.) It's 150 steps down to the mailbox, 150 steps back. I net another 95 steps walking around the cul-de-sac. It was 382 steps into my polling place during the primary (but that's useless information considering I don't need to go there very often). A big weekly grocery shopping trip, up and down most of the aisles and back out to the car, is about 1,400—especially because I always forget the onions and have to fight my way back through the produce department right before I check out.

It's kind of easy to fixate about the pedometer numbers. Walking around the baseball field is about .18 of a mile, or 465 steps. Picking up my daughter at school, if I park in the lower lot and walk to the gym, it's 130 steps one way. Going to visit a relative in an assisted living complex, which I do several times a week, gets me 100 steps on those long hallways. I can do 29 steps walking from the kitchen to the den to the living room to the dining room, which might not seem like a lot, but if I do it continuously while I'm on the phone, then I get more than 100.

And every time I take 100 steps, I'm another 1 percent closer to the total I need for the day.

Most people, I believe, would be similarly sucked in by the pedometer, which makes it a great tool for activity and weight loss. If nothing else, if I notice a low number around 5 p.m., it gives me a little nudge to get moving during whatever time remains in the day. I want to see the daily totals trend upward (it stores data for 7 previous days), and I don't think I'm alone in wanting this.

Michele's tip is to *not* wear a pedometer during exercise. Wear it for the rest of the day and try to get that number up. Here's why: It's common that people will start an exercise program and then diminish their other activity after they finish exercising. A pedometer can prevent that. Most people take 3,000 to 5,000 steps a day, not counting exercise. Make sure you get at least that and aim for more if you want faster weight loss results

Give one a try to see where you stand. Or, more to the point, see where you walk.

The daily workout remains the place where you can get the most steps in the least amount of time. On to the Stage 9 workout (opposite). There are a few twists this week, so read carefully!

As you can see, there are some shifts here. First, your total walking time is up to 2 hours 35 minutes at a minimum. It's significantly more than when you started, which is great. Kudos to you for making it this far, and I hope you'll take a minute to notice how far your abilities have progressed in just about 2 months.

Second, the speed walk continues to develop in intensity. Although the total fast walking time in this stage, 20 minutes, is only 2 minutes longer than the previous stage, with a 9-minute segment at the start of each workout, you're extending the fast-walking interval. These 9 minutes are a significant building block, getting you toward the time when you'll go 25 minutes fast without interruption. We hope, too, that the variation in the length of the fast walks will be a nice twist for you to keep your interest.

Remember, there should be a noticeable shift between your brisk walk speed and your fast walk speed. And whatever speed you're at for the beginning of the fast walk segment, try to hold that pace for all 9 minutes and, subsequently, for the 6-minute and 5-minute intervals. You want to be consistently faster. Simply put, this fast walking is what makes you lean and zaps calories.

The third change this week is the uptick in the challenge walk. It

WALK YOUR BUTT OFF!

STAGE 9

Minimum: 5 walks
Strength workouts*: 2–3 times this week

2 TO 4 BRISK WALKS

After warming up by walking at an easy pace for 2 to 3 minutes, you should walk at a purposeful pace, as if you need to get to an appointment, about 3 to 4 mph, for 30 to 40 minutes. Do a minimum of 2 brisk walks this week; a maximum of 4 if you're trying to walk every day.

Total workout time: 32–43 minutes

2 SPEED WALKS

➤ Start with a 2-minute warm-up at an easy pace.

➤ Then do 1 minute at a brisk pace, 9 minutes at a fast pace, 1 minute at a brisk pace, 6 minutes at a fast pace, 1 minute at a brisk pace, and 5 minutes at a fast pace.

➤ End with 3 minutes of easy walking.

Total fast walking time: 20 minutes.
Total workout time: 28 minutes.

1 CHALLENGE WALK

➤ Start with a 5-minute warm-up (2 minutes easy, 3 minutes brisk).

➤ Then do 15 minutes as fast as you can, noting your starting point and finishing point or distance.

➤ Return and walk back to the start at a more comfortable pace.

Total workout time: At least 35 minutes

For the strength workout, see page 75.

will feel harder to test yourself over 15 minutes at top speed versus 10. The same rules apply: Try to walk the same course week in and week out, and make a note of where you start and where you finish. You'll be doing this challenge walk for the rest of the program, so it's great to have a sense of your continued improvement.

Sometimes, as training becomes more intense, you may find you need more time to warm up, especially for the speed walks. If that's the case, you can lengthen your warm-up to 5 or even 10 minutes. Be sure, however, that you are gradually increasing your pace as the time ticks by, so that you are ready to walk fast when your warm-up is over. Try to add more time to the faster-paced part of your warm-up than to the easy walking in the very beginning.

Okay, listen up: It's time to turn off your headphones for just a minute to get the most out of this Technique Tip. Do you land with heavy, plopping footfalls, or are you relatively agile and silent? If you're not sure, ask a walking partner to come along and listen to your stride.

Tune in to the sounds your feet make. If they're consistently quiet, that's good news. If you make uneven sounds—louder with one foot than with the other—that could be a sign of injury or an imbalance. And if you're tromping like you're on snowshoes, then try to review the footstrike Technique Tips in Chapters 4, 5, and 6.

TECHNIQUE TIP #8

Be light on your feet

As I mentioned earlier, you should land on your heel, roll through your foot, and push off with your toes. During this stage, I want you to focus on landing softly and quietly. You want a smooth, quiet stride—not bouncing or plodding along—to go faster and reduce your risk of injury.

FOOD TALK:
MAKING DINNER MATTER

Dinner. It's a central part of the day, right? A time for families to get together, catch up, chat, and nourish their bodies and their relationships.

We've got all sorts of dinner ideals. Like the romantic ideal: a couple seated at a dining room table with linen tablecloth, china, crystal, candles lit, a salad course, main course, dessert, and fine wine. Then there's the family ideal: Mom, Dad, Junior, and Juniorette sitting down together, faces washed (okay, maybe that's only *my* fantasy), nice table manners, sharing the best and worst parts of their day, and supporting each other over a meal of healthy food.

Where are we really? Well, both the contents of our plates (if we even use them) and the quality of our conversations (if we have any) are lacking. We're driving through Chick-fil-A on the way to or from soccer practice. We've got tricky teenagers and stressed-out parents who bring their smartphones to the table like they're forks and napkins. We've got picky eaters swirling their vegetables around the plate as if painting Van Gogh's *The Starry Night* while their parents bargain, "Just have a bite of broccoli and then you can have dessert."

Never enough time to cook and eat. Never enough money to produce a healthy meal. Never enough family members around to help and sit down together. Or so it seems. Instead of being an oasis, dinner is a major stress of the day, something to "get through" on our way to plopping down on the couch in front of the TV. This dinner anxiety has spawned the Family Dinner Project at thefamilydinnerproject.org, a self-described "grassroots movement about food, fun, and conversation about things that matter" and that is dedicated to helping families solve these dilemmas.

Make a few small changes at the dinner hour, and you can vastly

Age: 48

Total weight lost:
Unchanged

Total inches lost:
2½ inches
from her waist

Walk time: **Faster by**
**1 minute
22 seconds**

Becca Kahle

How I got here: I've walked for exercise on and off for years. Since the boys were born, I haven't done very much. I go in spurts, but I am not able to be consistent. In 2008, I was diagnosed with breast cancer. Today, I am cancer free, and I want to develop a healthier lifestyle for myself and my boys.

Big wins: I've been tracking my walks with the RunKeeper app on my iPhone, and I'm sure when we go on vacation this summer, I'll be able to keep up with our friends and my mom, who is 72. In terms of eating, I've always sat down for 30 minutes and planned the family meals for the week. Now I'm focusing on getting more protein. I've switched from an oatmeal bar at breakfast to yogurt and granola. I'll pack lunch instead of buying it at work. I'm trying to cut back on the potatoes at dinner.

Next steps: Nighttime eating can be a problem for me. It's sort of haphazard. Leslie told me to plate it, bowl it, put it in a glass just so there's an upper limit on what I eat. I eat at night not because I'm hungry but from habit. I like the idea of keeping a list of appropriate snacks in the cabinet and going off that. Lately I've been able to stick to apples and clementines.

The long view: I didn't put on that extra 30 pounds in 12 weeks, so there was no way I was going to take it off in 12 weeks. I definitely came away smarter about how to walk to get the most bang for my buck and how to eat better. I also learned that it is okay if you can't walk or if you have a bad day eating. Just start where you are and look forward. I held on to my new habits and lost 8 pounds after the test panel ended.

improve the quality of what you eat and the quality of the time you spend. Here are Leslie's tips:

- Tweak the look of your plate so vegetables—and fruit, if you prefer— occupy half of it. That leaves plenty of room for a protein but minimizes the starch. "Usually something other than vegetables and fruit is front and center," Leslie says. "There's an entire fowl on the plate or a trough of pasta, and the fruits and vegetables are hanging on for dear life." Try flipping that ratio around. A little less pasta, a little more sauce with meat, and extra veggies added in. A stir-fry with vegetables and meat but not so much rice.

- Plan your dinners ahead of time for the week. Shop for your ingredients. On busy nights, make something fast; on nights when you have more time, do a slightly more elaborate meal. Prep on weekends or make enough of something to last for two meals. Think about dinner in advance the same way you plan your workouts. Keep healthy frozen options around for unforeseen scheduling challenges.

- Give eating dinner the attention it deserves. It's fine if you miss a few meals at home because of different schedules. But see if there are at least 3 nights a week when everyone can get together (and not in a car), even if that means pushing back dinner until 7:30 or later. Sit down at a table, turn off the TV, take the phone off the hook, and banish all cell phones.

WALK FAST; EAT SLOW!

Perhaps we should take a step back.

Before you start thinking about how you would like your dinnertime to be, think first about how quickly you eat. It's probably too fast.

Here's why: The body needs time to process fullness. If you're shoveling your food in quickly, you can overeat before your brain even gets the signal from the gut that a meal is incoming. Before you know it, you're stuffed. It takes about 20 minutes for the brain and the gut to get on the same wavelength.

Also, eating that fast simply isn't healthy—or comfortable—for digestion. Better to spread it out a little, and your gut will thank you for the slower pace. For breakfast, try to take 10 minutes. For lunch, try to take at least 15 minutes—extricate yourself from anything work related and use the time to nourish yourself. If you want to veg out and read *Us Weekly* while you're eating, fine, but don't attempt to multi-task lunch with anything that causes you more stress. For dinner, 20 minutes or longer is the ideal, but 15 is acceptable. (Five minutes is unacceptable.)

Aim to chew your food thoroughly. Taste it. Enjoy it! Take a few extra minutes to pay attention to the flavors and the texture. Other tips:

- **Put your fork down between bites.** Chew and swallow before picking up your utensils again.

- **Talk to your dinner mates.** It's not polite to talk with your mouth full, so conversation should slow you down.

- **Serve the salad first, like at a restaurant.** Then get up and serve the main course. Reclaim the dining room as a place for a meal.

- **If you're heading for seconds, take a break.** Stop eating for a minute and then reassess. Are you really still hungry?

CANS, PANS, *and* POUCHES

HEALTHY DINNER ON THE TABLE, PRONTO!

Leslie's recipe ideas here can help you get a well-balanced, healthy meal on the table quickly. She's not much of a cook, and her kids are grown, so I asked a friend—who is a mom of two young kids, a runner, and a pastry chef who trained at the French Culinary Institute—to test these ideas.

Roasted Vegetables with Sausage and Rotini

SERVES 4

1 pound turkey sausage

1 zucchini, sliced

6–8 mushrooms, sliced

2 cups chopped broccoli

1 red bell pepper, chopped

1 tablespoon olive oil plus additional for seasoning

Sea salt

Black pepper

½ pound whole wheat rotini pasta

Chili pepper flakes (optional)

Preheat the oven to 450°F. Line a cookie sheet with aluminum foil. Remove the casings from the sausage and coarsely chop. In a large nonstick skillet over medium-high heat, brown the sausage, then set aside. In a bowl, toss the zucchini, mushrooms, broccoli, and bell pepper with the oil and a pinch of salt and black pepper. Place the vegetables on the cookie sheet and roast for 10 minutes, or until tender. Meanwhile, cook the pasta according to package directions. Drain and set aside. Add the vegetables and sausage to the pasta. Season with pepper flakes, if desired, and a dash of oil.

Baked Tilapia with Spring Vegetables

SERVES 4

4 (6-ounce) pieces tilapia or other white fish

1 teaspoon plus 2 tablespoons olive oil

Lemon juice

1 teaspoon chopped parsley plus additional for seasoning

2 cloves garlic, minced

8 mushrooms, sliced

1 zucchini, sliced

1 green bell pepper, seeded and sliced

1 can (14 ounces) flavored diced tomatoes

Salt

Black pepper

1 mango, sliced

Preheat the oven to 350°F. Line a baking sheet with aluminum foil and place the fish on top. Brush with 1 teaspoon of the oil, then top with a splash of lemon juice and sprinkle with the parsley. Bake for 10 minutes, or until cooked through. Meanwhile, in a large nonstick skillet, heat the remaining 2 tablespoons oil over medium-high heat, and add the garlic, mushrooms, zucchini, and bell pepper. Sauté for 5 to 7 minutes, or until tender. Add the tomatoes and heat through.

Divide the vegetables among 4 plates, spooning them into the center of each plate. Cover with a piece of fish and season to taste with parsley, salt, and black pepper. Serve with sliced mango.

Chicken Rice Bowl

1⅓ cups cooked quick brown rice, such as Uncle Ben's Boil-in-Bag or Minute Rice

Baby spinach leaves

1 pound chicken breast, grilled and cut into strips*

1 cup fresh or canned pineapple chunks

2 tablespoons bottled salad dressing of your choice, such as a light red wine or raspberry vinaigrette

Place the rice in the bottom of a serving bowl. Top with the spinach (as much as desired), chicken, pineapple, and dressing.

Grill the chicken yourself or buy pregrilled chicken strips in the meat department at your grocery store.

Shrimp Stir-Fry

SERVES 4

2 10-ounce bags frozen baby shrimp, thawed

2 tablespoons olive oil

2 tablespoons minced ginger*

2 tablespoons finely chopped chile pepper*

6 cups frozen Asian-style vegetables

In a large nonstick skillet or wok over medium-high heat, add the shrimp and cook for 2 to 3 minutes. Set aside. In the same skillet or wok, add the oil, ginger, pepper, and vegetables and sauté for about 5 minutes, or until cooked. Add the shrimp and heat through. Serve over rice or noodles.

Or try Gourmet Garden Ginger Spice Blend and Chili Spice Blend

Salmon Burgers

SERVES 4

1 pound ground salmon*

1 bag (10 ounces) frozen chopped spinach, thawed and drained well

⅓ cup feta cheese crumbles

4 whole wheat sandwich thins

4 teaspoons mustard

Coat a grill rack with nonstick spray and preheat the grill. In a mixing bowl, combine the salmon, spinach, and feta. Mix well and form into 4 patties. Grill the patties for 5 minutes per side. Serve on a sandwich thin with a thin spread of mustard. Have with a salad of mixed greens and sliced apple, with raspberry vinaigrette.

Ask the butcher to grind the salmon just as you would get ground turkey.

Grilled Skirt Steak

SERVES 4

⅓ cup soy sauce

⅓ cup orange juice

2 cloves garlic, minced

1 teaspoon coarse kosher salt

1 pound skirt steak

2 sweet potatoes

Sliced tomatoes

Sliced cucumbers

Whisk together the soy sauce, orange juice, garlic, and salt in a large bowl. Add the steak and marinate for 2 to 3 hours. Remove from the marinade and grill or broil for about 5 minutes per side. While the steak is cooking, microwave the potatoes for 5 to 7 minutes, then turn and cook for 5 to 7 minutes longer. Cut the steak into ¼"-thick slices. Peel and mash the potatoes. Serve with the tomatoes and cucumbers.

Frittata

SERVES 4

1 tablespoon olive oil

1 cup baby spinach

1 zucchini, sliced

1 cup sliced mushrooms

1 green bell pepper, sliced

Minced garlic

8 eggs

Italian seasoning

Salt

Black pepper

Parmesan cheese, grated

In a large nonstick skillet, heat the oil over medium-high heat. Add the spinach, zucchini, mushrooms, pepper, and garlic to taste and sauté until cooked. Separately, beat the eggs with 2 tablespoons water, then add the Italian seasoning, salt, and pepper to taste. Pour the eggs over the vegetables and let cook until set, for 10 to 15 minutes. Sprinkle with the Parmesan to taste. Serve with sliced fruit.

Asian Salad

SERVES 4

1 bag (14 ounces) coleslaw (discard the dressing)

1 can (15 ounces) mandarin oranges, drained

2 cooked skinless, boneless chicken breasts, shredded

4 tablespoons chopped peanuts

2 green onions, diced

½ red bell pepper, chopped

4 tablespoons Asian sesame dressing

Toss the coleslaw with the oranges, chicken, peanuts, green onions, and pepper. Add the dressing and toss to combine.

Fish Tacos

SERVES 4

- - - - - - - -

4 6-ounce fillets of haddock, cod, or other thick white fish

Cajun seasoning, such as Chef Paul Prudhomme's Blackened Redfish Magic or McCormick's

8 tablespoons black bean dip, such as Guiltless Gourmet

4 (6" to 7") whole wheat tortillas

Shredded lettuce

Salsa

Coat the fish fillets with Cajun seasoning to taste. In a nonstick skillet over high heat, blacken the fish and continue heating until cooked through, about 5 minutes per side, depending on the thickness.

Meanwhile, spread 2 tablespoons of the black bean dip on each tortilla. Sprinkle with shredded lettuce. Cut the fish into thin strips and divide among the tortillas. Top with salsa to taste and roll the tortillas.

Tuna, Bean, and Salsa Salad

SERVES 4

- - - - - - - -

2 cans (6 ounces each) tuna, packed in olive oil

1 can (15 ounces) cannellini beans, drained and rinsed

1 cup fresh salsa

4 whole grain rolls

Drain the tuna and place in a medium bowl. Mix in the beans and salsa. Serve with the rolls or a 3"-long piece of whole grain baguette.

To-Do List

☐ Take a look at your calendar to plan at least five times you can walk during the next week.

☐ Complete at least five workouts, including at least 2 brisk walks, 2 speed walks, and your first 15-minute challenge walk. Don't schedule speed walks and/or challenge walks on back-to-back days. Make a note of how far you go during your challenge walk.

☐ Complete at least two sets of strength exercises on nonconsecutive days.

☐ Think about how fast you eat. Try different strategies to eat a little more slowly at each meal. As you're eating, think about how full you are.

☐ Plan your dinners for the upcoming week. When can you eat at home? When do you need to eat on the road? When do you have time to cook, and when do you have to get a meal on the table fast?

☐ Optional: Order a pedometer to track your steps for a week at a time when you're not working out. Where can you add a few more steps?

Lorraine Wiedorn-------

Age: 51

Height: 5'1"

Total pounds lost:
4.4 *pounds*
in 12 weeks

Total inches lost:
5¼ *inches*,
including 2¼ inches
from her waist and
1½ inches from her hips

Starting walk time:
17:19

Ending walk time:
14:34

Faster by:
2 minutes
45 seconds

Before

Day job: Assistant vice president, Office of Planned Giving, at a university; married, mother of two children ages 21 and 16

How I got here: I've been married for 25 years, and in those years, after two children, I've gained 20 pounds. I don't have poor eating habits. I don't sit down and eat a tub of ice cream. Life got busy. When you're working and raising a family and driving kids here and there, the one thing you cut out is doing things for yourself.

How I started: Now that my children are grown, I am coming back to taking care of myself. Now I feel like I have a little more time, and I'm getting back into setting time aside for me.

Winning strategies: I am very much schedule-driven to begin with. I figured out right away, based on my schedule, when I can fit this in. I know that on Monday, I can do it before I go to work. On Tuesday, in the morning, I do the Pilates tape, and I drive my daughter to school because she can't take her French horn on the bus. Tuesday night I walk. I like that. That is what has gotten me to be so consistent in my routine. I have it all plotted out.

I like the speed walks. I take my cell phone out, and I hit the timer button. It's right there. It's instant gratification. You're doing it, you're out of breath, and then it's "Okay, now I can walk for a minute and catch my breath." Do it again for 10 minutes. I like that.

Big wins: In my youth, I was very strong. I could do 50 pushups on the floor. Now I'm getting back to that, and it makes me feel good. I did 10 on the car bumper, and now I'm back to 10 on the floor.

I'm a little disappointed I lost only 4 pounds, but I have to realize there are no quick fixes.

Workout mind-set: When I walk at night, I walk with my neighbor. I give her lots of credit for helping me do this. On the days when I can't get out before I go to work, it's 8 at night, and in the winter, it's cold and already dark. I call Eileen or she will call me: "Are we walking?" Deep breath. "Yeah, we're walking."

Nutrition pointers that worked: I had stopped eating breakfast. Now I make a point of eating breakfast— a bowl of cereal or some yogurt with granola. Every week, I will hard-cook three eggs. I'll have a piece of toast and a hard-cooked egg, and I'm satisfied until lunch. Leslie helped me see that it's important to have a decent snack around 4, so I'll slice an apple and put some peanut butter on it.

We sit down together for dinner around 7 o'clock. That is our time to reconnect. No cell phones at the table. If the phone rings, we don't answer it. It's just a lot of fun. Everybody talks about the day, and it's just our time. We've always done that. We probably spend anywhere from half an hour to 40 minutes at the dinner table.

Best advice: You should have a plan. You need to plug it into your schedule. That's what the program has forced me to do. You've got to be disciplined about it. If it's important to you, you're going to do it. This is important to me, so I do it.

CHAPTER 10

Staying ON Course

Best I can tell, there are two types of people in the world: those who hit the "snooze" button on the alarm clock and those who don't.

I've been a member of both camps—sometimes even in the same week. On a Monday, I'll bounce out of bed in the morning without a moment's hesitation and have my workout clothes on before I reach the bathroom. By Wednesday, I'm rolling over and pulling the covers over my head, postponing the inevitable, until it's too late to think about doing a workout before the day starts. The opportunity is lost.

Motivation is a tricky thing. The internal tank of get-up-and-go is different for everyone. Although some folks never seem to falter in their discipline, they're rare. Others go through focused periods, with their eyes on a personal prize. Then their supply of enthusiasm ebbs to the point where they collapse back onto the couch, sometimes for weeks at a time.

Even the most driven among us have anti-Nike days, when we Just *Don't* Do It. We look at our exercise gear at the end of a stressful workday and rationalize why we deserve a day off from walking. The workout doesn't happen. We don't want to go.

As the program nears its conclusion, you should think ahead about your own level of motivation. What's going to keep you moving this week and next month? Our test panelists all said that e-mailing their workouts to Coach Michele and me and knowing they were going to get weighed were powerfully motivating forces. But the reality is, after the program ended, some stopped walking regularly, while others continued and pushed farther and faster.

So what works for you? What doesn't? Stage 10, when the newness of the program has worn off, is a good time to start thinking about your motivational techniques and develop new ones if you need a kick in the pants. You're more than 2 months into this routine, with a lifetime ahead of you. What's going to make regular walking exercise stick as a part of your daily routine?

THOUGHTS TO GET YOU GOING

I asked the test panelists to share how they kept going on their I-don't-really-want-to days. Here's what Becca Kahle thinks about on days she doesn't feel like walking:

"I would remember my vacation 2 years ago. We were visiting friends in Saugatuck, Michigan. In order to get to the beaches on Lake Michigan, you had to walk up hundreds of stairs, then go down stairs. I kept having to stop to catch my breath. So here I am with old friends, and I can barely walk up the stairs. It was embarrassing. We'd like to visit them again, and I want to be able to easily go up and down those stairs. I know if I walk now, even when I don't want to, I'll have a different result next time. That's what I think about to motivate myself."

Steve Cobb is with her. "I remind myself how I felt before I started the program: I couldn't bend down to tie my shoes without a lot of effort. I had no energy. Those memories get me up and moving."

Crystal Dye had her wedding as motivation. "There were many times I felt like I didn't want to walk in the cold," she said. "I would remind myself of how good I'd feel after I finished my walk. I knew I would be happy and proud of my accomplishment. Plus, the accountability of logging my walks kept me motivated. And my wedding dress did not have to be let out in the hip area, thanks to those power walks!"

THE BUDDY SYSTEM

Okay, so we don't all have a wedding to train for. Sometimes we have to put other systems—or people—in place to hold us going. Donna Karoly had some not-too-subtle friends keep her accountable. "I had a buddy at work that pushed me and a friend at the gym that would meet me to walk," she says. "Both would tell me, 'Get your butt moving.' And they still do. Today at work, we did six laps around the inside of our building because it is raining. We also have a couple of teams that walk at lunch, so I always have motivation (and sometimes guilt) to get out and walk."

Unwitting motivators are everywhere; you just have to find them. It might be the injured war vet who would love to exercise but can't. One runner I interviewed a few years ago, a teacher in Florida, told me how a student motivated her. The girl was battling cancer and missed nearly half the days in a school year for treatment. Yet she managed to get every assignment in on time. Years after the girl's death, the teacher remained inspired by her student's commitment. "If Tanya could get her homework in on time, through chemotherapy and radiation, I could do the required training for a marathon," she said.

MUNDANE MOTIVATORS

What helps me is far more ordinary than a walking buddy or an inspirational person: I leave my workout clothes in a pile on the floor next to the bed. That's right. I have to go by them on my way to the bathroom, so they are hard to ignore. I've heard of people who put Post-it Notes on their bathroom mirrors with motivational messages. Mine just takes the form of laundry instead.

Find a Friend and Walk for Life

In May 2012, I happened to sit down at a wedding next to Brenda Krushinski, a mutual friend of the bride. Brenda, a teacher and mother of three, started telling me about her walking routine and a friendship that developed from it. After the wedding, she e-mailed me the details of their walks.

"I made the commitment to walk 5 years ago. I love watching and playing sports, but I had back surgery when I was younger, so I can't run. I have to prioritize my health and take care of myself so I can take care of the three little people who depend on me. That's why I decided to start walking.

A colleague told me about Jenn Kearney. We met, clicked, and found out that we lived in the same neighborhood. We work part-time in special education, and we have three kids almost the same ages.

When we first started walking together, our commitment level was slightly different. It wasn't unusual for us to miscommunicate about whether we were walking the next day, so I'd bring my iPod in case I was alone. We are now both committed. Texting to confirm makes things easy.

During the week, we walk from 6:15 to 7 a.m., then a quick shower and get the kids off to school. On the weekends, it's more like 60 to 90 minutes (4 to 6 miles) on one of the 2 days. I *hate* cold, so in the past, we've hibernated from about November to March. This year was the first year that Jenn and I walked through the winter.

We live at opposite ends of two streets that are parallel to each other, so we leave and meet on the adjoining street. Occasionally, one of us is running late, so we walk toward the other's house until we meet up. Sometimes, it's so dark and quiet that we don't see each other until we're 5 feet away. Then we scream and laugh and say, "Thank God it's you!"

We chat the entire time and never run out of things to talk about. Through the years, we've each experienced trying times, and our walks have become, as we call it, our therapy. Walking has been beneficial in so many ways, both physically and emotionally. Jenn and I also do daily problem solving; having six kids with activities after school, sometimes our walks are times for us to figure out our arrangements or ways to help each other. We truly enjoy each other's company. I know that if we didn't make this commitment to each other, I would be much less likely to get out. I know Jenn feels the same.

Coach Michele recommends making a list of all the reasons you want to exercise. Be as specific as possible. For example, to be able to run and play with your kids or grandkids, to have more energy when you get home from work, to feel confident enough to wear your shirt tucked into your pants. Anytime you're contemplating skipping a workout or have already gotten off track, pull out the list to review it for a motivation boost.

In fact, we'll leave some space right here for you to make some notes on why you want to exercise:

_____

_____

_____

_____

SOCIAL MEDIA AND "JUST 5 MINUTES"

Some friends have told me they e-mail each other from across the country several times a week to compare notes on their exercise. The thought of that buddy getting out there is enough to rev up an idle engine. Other pairs work out at the same time in different locations and talk on the phone as they're starting so they know they're there. Groups of runners and walkers congregate on social media sites like Dailymile (dailymile.com) to encourage each other. Gayle Hendricks blogs about her walking.

On the days when motivation hits its lowest point, there's the "just 5 minutes" rationale. It goes like this: "I'll just start working out for 5 minutes, I'll go slow, and if I feel terrible, I promise I'll go home." The first few steps are the hardest, but by 5 minutes, you usually feel a little better. So you bargain with yourself for another 5. By then, you're 10 minutes into a 30-minute workout, so if you can make it 5 more, you're halfway there. See where this leads?

Figure out which motivational techniques work best for you. Some people rely on a combination of strategies, and the strategies evolve over time. In the end, it's the consistency of exercising 5 days a week, week after week, month after month, that is going to help you feel better, get lean, and *stay* lean.

The Stage 10 workout is on the next page. For motivation, know that this set of walks brings you closer to the final goal of 25 minutes, nonstop, at a fast pace. For motivation, look back to Stage 2 to see how far you've come.

As you've been doing with all the challenge walks, note your start point and end point. You should be able to cover close to a mile—and some people will be able to smash the 1-mile barrier—in 15 minutes. Test panelist Deb Davies did her final speed walk in 12 minutes and covered a mile, so if she had maintained that pace for 15 minutes, she'd be at $1\frac{1}{4}$ miles. The speed walk allows you to cover a lot of ground in a short, intense period of time.

This Technique Tip might seem odd. It's like doing those dreaded Kegel exercises—no one can tell you're doing them. But squeezing your glutes for a few minutes during every walk will help you become firmer in the posterior. You will, in fact, walk your butt off.

TECHNIQUE TIP # 9

• Squeeze your glutes

Each time your heel lands on the ground, squeeze your buttock muscles. Imagine that you're using those muscles to pull your body forward over your front leg. Practice this periodically (a minute or so at a time) during your warmup, brisk walk, and cooldown.

STAGE *10*

Minimum: 5 walks
Strength workouts*: 2–3 times this week

2 TO 4 BRISK WALKS

After warming up by walking at an easy pace for 2 to 3 minutes, you should walk at a purposeful pace, as if you need to get to an appointment, about 3 to 4 mph, for 30 to 40 minutes. Do a minimum of 2 brisk walks this week; a maximum of 4 if you're trying to walk every day.

Total workout time: 32–43 minutes

2 SPEED WALKS

➤ Start with a 2-minute warm-up at an easy pace.
➤ Then do 1 minute at a brisk pace, 12 minutes at a fast pace, 1 minute at a brisk pace, 10 minutes at a fast pace.
➤ End with 3 minutes of easy walking.

Total fast walking time: 22 minutes.
Total workout time: 29 minutes.

1 CHALLENGE WALK

➤ Start with a 5-minute warm-up (2 minutes easy, 3 minutes brisk).
➤ Then do 15 minutes as fast as you can, noting your starting point and finishing point or distance.
➤ Return and walk back to the start at a more comfortable pace.

Total workout time: At least 35 minutes

For the strength workout, see page 75.

Small Step for Success

Here is one easy trick to ensure you get your walk in: Keep a pair of sneakers in your car. (If you're an urban dweller, carry your sneakers in a backpack with you at all times.) That way, if you're faced with an unexpected delay somewhere, you can walk a little. Do a lap around the grocery store parking lot before heading in to shop—or do it after shopping if you don't have perishables. Instead of driving back home after dropping kids off at piano lessons, walk in that area. Walk to do an errand instead of driving. If a lunchtime conference call gets rescheduled, put those sneakers on and head out. Even if you can't fit in the full workout, some is better than none. A short workout will keep your momentum going.

The move will also give you more strength to propel you forward, faster, over time. Just as you can power your stride by pushing off your rear foot, squeezing your glutes adds to your speed and power. With strong glutes, your fast pace—whether it's 4, 4.5, or 5 miles per hour—is easier to maintain and improve upon.

FOOD TALK:
FIBER, COLOR, AND RESTAURANT DINING

So far, we've asked you to look at protein, liquid, breakfast, lunch, dinner, and snacks. Fiber is the last "ingredient" in a healthy daily diet that we're asking you to scrutinize.

Why fiber? Lots of reasons.

- **You have to chew foods with fiber in them.** That makes them satisfying. Chewing burns a few calories and gives your mouth something productive to do.

- **Your body holds more water when it's digesting fibrous foods.** The water combined with the fiber keeps you fuller longer.

- **High-fiber foods don't digest as easily.** In other words, they hang around in the stomach longer, adding to the time you feel full.

- **Fiber itself is not an energy source for the human body—it just passes on through.** So there are two benefits here. When you eat foods with fiber, there's a lower calorie count to those foods but still usually big taste and chew. Second, the body expends a little more energy breaking down fibrous foods, so you burn calories digesting it without even realizing it. This is what scientists call the "thermogenic effect" of food.

Convinced? Good. Here's where to find fiber:

- Fruits and vegetables, like raspberries and artichokes, can boost your fiber while you satisfy your sweet or salty cravings.

- Legumes (beans, peas, and lentils) are loaded with fiber.

- Grains, like barley, especially those that include bran, can be rich sources of fiber. (Read the labels to be sure!) Get your grain dose from breads, cereals, and pastas. Popcorn and nuts, like almonds, also carry fiber to the body.

Rather than having all your fiber at one time, try to get a little with each meal of the day. So maybe a bran cereal with a piece of fruit at breakfast, a vegetable-rich soup at lunch along with more fruit, and plenty of veggies with dinner. Fiber is part of the reason why Leslie encourages people to compose half their plate with vegetables at dinner. It's not only about the vitamins and nutrients, it's about the fiber, which may prove more filling than you would have predicted.

So how much fiber do you need?

Women and men younger than age 50 need 25 to 38 grams of fiber per day. People older than 50 need 21 to 30 grams a day. That's a lot. An apple has 2.5 grams of fiber (almost as much as a whole McDonald's Big

Mac, which has 3 grams). Eating a bean burrito from Taco Bell gets you a little closer with 10 grams, but don't forget about all the fat, calories, and sugar that come along with it. Suddenly, it's easy to see why most Americans—at least those who haven't been paying attention to their diets—don't get anywhere near the recommended amount.

So for you, the first step is to do a quick count to see how much fiber you're currently getting. Go back to your most recent food log, pencil in the grams of fiber next to each food, and tally it up. If you don't have a label handy, you can often find it online at the brand's Web site. Or a basic calorie counting site will display the amount of fiber in each food along with all the other nutrition information such as calories and grams of protein.

Two caveats: If you're not getting the fiber you need, add it to your diet gradually, that is, at the rate of about 5 additional grams per week. (So if you're currently getting 15 grams a day, try to nudge it up to 20, then hold it at that rate for a week before adding another 5.) Too much fiber all at once can cause GI distress, which you want to avoid, especially when you're out on a walk miles from your house!

Second, as you build your fiber intake, continue consuming plenty of fluids to keep the fiber movin' through your system and not sitting in your gut.

Getting fiber is pretty easy. If you think about changing your white foods to brown foods and adding a colorful item to every meal—breakfast and lunch, too, not just dinner—you'll go a long way toward getting the fiber you need. Plus, you'll benefit from the vitamins, nutrients, and fluid those foods provide.

How might this look?

Breakfast: Swap out your Kellogg's Special K (0 gram of fiber) for General Mills' Multi-Bran Chex (6 grams of fiber). Add ½ cup of blueberries for an additional 1.8 grams, and you're almost to 10 grams for the morning. **Total: 9.8 grams of fiber**

Snack: Trade your Snyder's of Hanover Snaps Pretzels (0.5 gram of fiber) for Newman's Own High Protein Pretzels (4 grams of fiber). Add ¹/₂ cup of edamame for 3.8 grams of fiber. **Total: 7.6 grams of fiber**

Lunch: Exchange your two pieces of white bread (1 gram of fiber for both) for a 10-inch whole wheat tortilla (6 grams of fiber). Throw in a side of baby carrots (2 grams of fiber in 14 sticks) or a pear with the skin (5.5 grams of fiber). **Total: 11.5 grams of fiber if you opt for the pear**

Dinner: With your chicken breast or salmon, have ¹/₄ cup of refried beans on the side (3.3 grams of fiber) or 1 cup of brown rice (3 grams of fiber) or a medium-size sweet potato (3.8 grams of fiber). Instead of an iceberg lettuce salad, opt for 1 cup of steamed broccoli (5 grams). **Total: Around 8 grams of fiber**

Total for the day: 36.9 grams

See? That's not so hard. With a few easy swaps, you can easily up your fiber total to where it needs to be. You'll find you feel fuller longer, and your mouth will stay happy, too, chewing it all up. Remember, don't make all these swaps in one day. Try adding them over a period of weeks.

A MORE COLORFUL PLATE

To focus on fruits and vegetables solely for the fiber they provide would be missing the forest for the trees. Colorful foods (and we're not talking about Trix, Skittles, or red wine) are chockful of vitamins and minerals, everything the cells of your body need for ideal functioning. The nutrients that come from plants and fruits help fight off illness; maintain strong bones, muscles, and teeth; and contribute to the liquid our bodies need in a day, as discussed in Chapter 8. (To review: That's 90 ounces for women and 125 for men.) The colorful foods will make your body work better, walk faster, and live healthier from head to toe.

Here are just a few examples from Leslie of the way fruits and vegetables can multitask:

Cherries and tart cherry juice: They reduce inflammation in the body and provide a natural source of melatonin to help regulate sleep.

Tomatoes: The lycopene in tomatoes may support bone health and is also an anti-inflammatory agent.

Plums, fresh or dried: They are chewy and sweet, which helps with satiety, and they promote bone health and digestive health.

Fresh or roasted soybeans: Soybeans (also labeled as edamame) are an excellent source of protein and can help lower cholesterol.

Spinach: Popeye's fave is helpful for eye health and heart health.

Dried beans: Legumes promote digestive health, heart health, and blood glucose control and have anti-inflammatory properties.

Sweet potatoes: These colorful spuds are a great source of fiber and can help lower blood glucose.

DON'T FORGET THE FREEZER CASE . . .

Or the canned food aisle. The sweet thing about produce is that you don't have to buy it fresh. I've had the experience of dropping a bundle of cash on veggies at our local farmers' market and then watched with dismay a few days later as the produce rotted in the fridge and fruit flies buzzed around the bowl on my counter.

Add a little produce to your diet week by week, and don't restrict your shopping to the fresh section at the front of the store. You can get canned tomatoes, beans, and mangos without losing any of the nutritional benefits. Buying frozen chopped onions, bell peppers, and other veggies can speed up a meal's prep time. Look for frozen berries to add to oatmeal or smoothies, especially when they're out of season.

STRIVE FOR FIVE

That slogan may be a marketing gimmick—strive for five servings of fruits and vegetables daily—but it's a good rule of thumb. As with any change to your diet or exercise program, however, it's fine to start gradually and build up. Here are a few ideas for how to do it:

Breakfast: Eat half a grapefruit, chop an apple on top of your oatmeal, throw some frozen berries into a smoothie, or put a dollop of salsa on top of your eggs.

Lunch: Spread hummus instead of mayo on your sandwich bread. Opt for half a sandwich and 1 cup of vegetable bean soup instead of a whole sandwich. Stuff baby spinach and bell peppers into a pita bread pocket for a sandwich. Pickles are vegetables, too. (*Yes!*)

Snacks: Pair the first ingredient of your snack with edamame, baby carrots, cherry tomatoes, or celery sticks, which will keep you chewing for a while. Or add frozen berries into plain Greek yogurt and top with a dab of honey. And you can't go wrong with an apple or a navel orange.

Dinner: To fill half your plate with vegetables, choose two of them for your meal—salad and steamed broccoli, for instance, or green beans and carrots. Add fruit such as pineapple or mango to your dinner, or toss a can of drained mandarin oranges into your spinach salad. If you're serving soup, stir in a cup of frozen mixed vegetables to amp up the nutrient content.

A CHANGE IN MIND-SET

It takes a lot of practice to start thinking about fruits and vegetables as go-to items when you're hungry. You have to have the stuff available and visible so you can see it when you're scrounging for a snack. It took me years to start bringing baby carrots in the car to nosh on instead of pretzels. I've started washing and hulling the fresh strawberries as soon as I get them home, which seems to make them last longer and certainly induces me to reach for them instead of a cookie. I'm trying to keep the cabinet where I store the packaged snacks closed and look elsewhere first. For the kids after school, I'll often defrost ¼ cup of frozen blueberries in the microwave and top them with a dollop of orange sherbet. They'll eat red bell pepper sticks with a tablespoon of ranch dressing while they're working on their homework.

I like to think we're saving hundreds of calories over the course of the day and doing a better job of meeting their growing bodies' nutritional needs. It's a work in progress, for sure.

ADD, NOT SUBTRACT

It's a lot more fun to think about what you can add to your diet than to constantly think about where you have to cut back. You can eat as many vegetables as you want. Fruits, too. Weight Watchers recognized this when it made fruits and vegetables free from their points system a few years back.

So turn the thinking on its head: Instead of deny, deny, deny—no cake, no chips, no soda—try thinking about what you can add. More protein, more fiber, more fruits, more vegetables. It's simply a happier way to think about eating. Plus, when you're eating all the protein and fiber you need, getting your 2½ cups of daily vegetables and 2 cups of fruit, you feel fuller. And your calorie total naturally falls in line with what it should be.

RESTAURANT EATING

Eating out is unavoidable, especially for busy families. So how can you deal? I quizzed Leslie about this, using my own family's habits as a guide for the questions.

Leslie, I know that two weeknights this week, part of the family will be out at meetings or practices. We'd normally grab a pizza or something. What should we do on those nights?

Leslie: *If you're getting a pizza to bring home, can you order one with a thin crust? Definitely have the pizzeria double-cut it, so instead of automatically having two full slices, you'll have one and* *a half. Or order the pizza with extra vegetable toppings.*

At the local diner, order a vegetable omelet, but hold the cheese. If you want a smaller portion, ask for it. If you want double veggies instead of a single veggie and a starch, ask for that, too. There are choices you can make. Split an entrée with the person you are dining with. Eat an appetizer as a main course so you're eating more like a kid.

Is it better to do part takeout, part cook at home than to sit down at a restaurant?

Leslie: *That's a solid strategy. Do a rotisserie chicken, a bag of prewashed salad, and a microwave pouch of brown rice. You'll come out far ahead in the nutrient total and far fewer in the calorie total than if you sit down to chicken, mashed potatoes, and green beans cooked to mushiness and coated with butter. If you eat at a Chinese restaurant, order your entrée steamed, like steamed chicken and vegetables. Ask for the brown sauce on the side. You'll eat far less if you spoon some on yourself than if the entire dinner is cooked in it. If it's too hard to resist the egg roll in the restaurant, have someone else call in the order and pick it up.*

What about the fancy places? You know, when we go out for "date night"?

Answer: *This is a tricky one. Just because it's a special night doesn't mean you should go hog wild. You can undo a lot of the hard work you've done walking and eating right throughout the week with one restaurant meal. But you still want it to feel like a special occasion.*

So you have to bargain with yourself. Ask them to hold the bread basket and bring your salad ASAP if you're really hungry. If you're at a place that's known for having the best dessert in town, by all means, you should have the dessert! But plan for it by passing on the roll and the potato. No one ever walks out of a restaurant saying, "That was the best darn baked potato I ever had."

To-Do List

☐ Take a look at your calendar to plan at least five times you can walk during the next week.

☐ Complete at least five workouts, including at least 2 brisk walks, 2 speed walks, and your second 15-minute challenge walk. Don't schedule speed walks and/or challenge walks on back-to-back days. Make a note of how far you go during your challenge walk. Did you cover more ground than you did during the previous stage?

☐ Complete at least two sets of strength exercises on nonconsecutive days.

☐ Analyze your current fiber intake. How close are you to meeting the minimum you need for your age? Where are some places where you can add more fiber to your diet?

☐ Think about fruits and vegetables: Which ones do you like? With which meals and snacks can you add an extra serving?

☐ How many meals do you eat out each week? Can you reduce that total by one? How can you make restaurant dining healthier for yourself and your family?

Age: 33

Height: 5'7"

Total pounds lost:
4.4 *pounds*
in 12 weeks

Total inches lost:
3½ *inches*,
including 2½ inches
from her waist

Starting walk time:
15:18

Ending walk time:
13:30

Faster by:
**1 minute
48 seconds**

Before

Crystal Dye --------------

Day job: Client relationship manager for a financial services firm. Married.

How I got here: My whole life, I struggled with my weight, even as a kid. My highest weight was 296 pounds. It was my second time back at Weight Watchers that something finally clicked. I lost 125 pounds and had kept it off for 5 years when I started the test panel. But those last 15 to 20 pounds are sticking.

How I started: When I started losing weight on my own, I walked for exercise. The most I could do was 10 minutes at about 3 miles per hour. It was a start.

Winning strategies: I discovered that if I drink tea, I don't need a sweet every night. Different flavored tea is my treat. I have stocked caramel vanilla and raspberry. It smells great, and it lasts a long time. I like quantity. I always want a lot of whatever I'm eating.

For another snack, I would spray popcorn with I Can't Believe It's Not Butter and then sprinkle it with seasoning. I found a kettle corn seasoning and a cinnamon French toast seasoning. I felt like I was snacking all night. It was great.

Scaling back: I only weigh in once a month at Weight Watchers. When I had a scale, I would sometimes weigh myself in the morning and again later that evening. It was insane. So I don't even own a scale anymore.

Workout mind-set: That exercise log would have those empty spaces, and I'd think, "Okay, I want to fill these in." There would be days when I'd be like, "Ugh, I'm not feeling it today." I'd tell myself, "C'mon, get dressed, put the clothes on, and go." After the first 5 to 7 minutes, I was in the mood. Then I was so happy I did it. The first couple of minutes were tough, but once I broke through that wall, I felt good.

Secret weapons: Friday nights, you want to feel like you're eating junk, so I try to trick my brain. I make cheese steak with lean meat and low-fat cheese on a wrap and bake sweet potato fries. I know if I go out and order those things, they're terrible for me.

Best advice: A lot of people ask me for advice, and I always say, when you come from 300 pounds and you struggle and you don't know anything, start with something small to change. Don't try to change everything, or it becomes overload. Just believe in yourself, that you're capable, and then do small bits. I started by getting rid of my deep fryer and walking 10 minutes daily.

CHAPTER 11

Walk
LIKE AN
Athlete

A few months after the 12-week test panel ended, I got an e-mail from participant Gayle Hendricks. She had just finished a 50-kilometer walk from White's Ferry, Maryland, to Harpers Ferry, West Virginia.

Fifty kilometers. That's 31.07 miles of walking. (And I take Gayle's word for it when she says if you've walked for 30 miles, you really feel that last mile!) She started with a friend at 10 a.m., and they finished just after 9 p.m. They were entrants in the One Day Hike, a noncompetitive event that's been happening since 1974 and that follows the Chesapeake & Ohio Canal path. "We did great for the first 24 miles, but the last 7 were tough," Gayle wrote. "We started at a 4-mile-per-hour pace, slowed to a 3, and probably finished closer to 2. The end was a steep, 2-mile hill. I dragged my sorry butt up that hill. And at the 30-mile mark, we had to climb stairs to a foot bridge."

The walk was the culmination of months of workouts Gayle had done in preparation. On weekdays, she would follow the schedule set forth by WYBO!, plus she would stand for 3 or 4 hours at a time while she was teaching. On weekends, she practiced walking for up to 90 minutes.

When you have a goal like hers, you can't slack off. Not if you hope to meet the challenge. When you have that date circled on the calendar, you have an extra nudge to find your sneakers and get out. The fear of embarrassment or failing to finish is a great inspiration to train. Spending money on an entry fee ups the ante, too. You don't want to waste your money if you are not able to walk.

Try it. You don't have to pick a 30-miler. I encourage you to find a walking event and sign up—and not just because it's motivational. Rather, because it's fun. You'll find when you get there that pinning on a number and being out among a group of people with like-minded goals is an uplifting experience. And it's great to chat with people you don't know, groan through the uphills, and high-five each other and share stories when it's over.

An event can make you feel like an athlete. Which, by now, you are.

I remember walking a New Year's Eve 5-K in Bethlehem, Pennsylvania, with a few members of the test panel. They were in Stage 9 of the program. I followed Susan DeSmet for almost all of the 3.1 total miles. Midway through, as her arms pumped away, the sweat started showing through the back of her shirt. By the end, she was soaked, athough her arms never slowed their rhythm. This sweet school nurse who wanted to lose a few pounds had morphed into someone unequivocally tough and athletic. When it was over, you could tell from the glow on her face how happy she was with her time (42:25) and her effort. Her husband, who walked with her, was really proud. He was glowing, too.

WALK FOR A CAUSE

Coach Michele enters events all the time. I e-mailed her one day with some walking questions, and when she got back to me, she happened to include her upcoming event schedule. Half-marathon in October, a 5-K in December, another half in April, one in May . . .

But her most memorable? "I'd have to say it was coming up to the finish line at the Avon Walk for Breast Cancer in Washington, DC, back in 2000," she says. "We walked about 20 miles each day for 3 days (the Avon walks are now 2 days), from Frederick, Maryland, to the Washington Monument. I decided to do the walk after a friend who was a 3-year breast cancer survivor had a relapse. It was my way to support her and honor my mom's sister, my dad's sister, and my husband's aunt, who all had survived breast cancer. I trained with my mom, and we walked it together.

"The organizers corralled all the walkers together about a half-mile or so from the finish so we could all finish together. When everyone was gathered, we started our walk down the Mall toward the Washington Monument. The cheers got louder as we continued, but the most incredible moment was when we created a path and all the breast cancer survivors who completed the 3-day walk filed past us. It was so empowering to see these strong women, some whose hair still hadn't grown back in after treatments, triumphing over both breast cancer and a 60-mile walk."

I get chills just reading Michele's description, so I can only imagine how it must have felt to see it and be part of it. Walking for a charitable cause is a great way to put your newfound fitness to use and is a compelling reason to walk on days you don't feel like training.

START SMALL

Convinced to give an event a try? Good. Look around for a 5-K. If you're worried that everyone else is running and you'll be walking—and therefore finish last—check out the results from the previous year to see where you would fit in. The more entrants there are, the greater range of finishing times you'll find.

How can you predict your time? Well, your challenge walk gives you some clue. Measure how far you get in 15 minutes. You can use your car's odometer to check the distance or you can invest in a higher-end GPS watch to tell you how far you've traveled in a workout.

Dave McGovern: Racewalker, Coach, and Seven-Time Olympic Trials Qualifier

"I'm the national walk coach for Team Challenge, the training and fund-raising program for the Crohn's and Colitis Foundation. My wife has colitis, so it's a passion of mine.

About a quarter of the people who join Team Challenge are purely walkers. They have no desire to try to run. They'll fund-raise for the foundation; we'll work with them and train them for 15 weeks to complete a half-marathon. Our motto is One Team, One Goal.

There are some people who look at Team Challenge as a weight loss program. Whatever someone's goal is, I'm going to try to help them reach it. If it's weight loss, you've got to add walking in with whatever you're already doing for fitness. You have to look at the week in totality. Yes, we're doing long walks on weekends to get ready for events. Some people get so beat up on their long walk, they need to recover from that for a few days. But if someone is trying to lose weight, I say you should try to walk every day. Go 7 days a week so you're burning calories every day. After all, you're taking calories in every day. Make time. There's always something else you can cut back on to find the time. Walking is good for your mind, body, and soul.

Normal walking technique is mechanically limiting. To get beginners going faster, number one, I have them focus on their arms. Elbows should be bent so your arms are swinging like a shorter, faster pendulum. Number two, shorten your stride but increase your stride frequency. Your speed is a product of stride length times stride frequency. The longer steps you take, that front foot gets in your way, like you're putting on the brakes. And finally, push off with the ball of your foot.

I've trained a lot of people who can walk a half-marathon in 3 hours (13:44 pace, or about 4.3 mph). And quite a few have bumped up against 2½ hours (11:27 pace, or 5.2 mph). They're faster than many runners, and that becomes part of the motivation: Let's see how many runners I can beat."

Learn more about Dave and Team Challenge at racewalking.org.

An iPhone gives you the same information, and certain Web sites, such as mapmyrun.com, will give you an accurate measurement, too.

Let's say you cover 1.1 miles in 15 minutes. If you were able to maintain that pace, 13 minutes 38 seconds per mile, then you'd cover 3.3 miles in 45 minutes. You won't be able to maintain your challenge walk pace for that long, so cut back your expectations some. Perhaps you'd cover the 3.1 miles in 45 minutes, a 14:30 per mile pace.

You won't know for sure until you try it for the first time. But know this: The adrenaline rush you get from being part of an event counts for a lot. It will propel you faster than you think you can go.

When you finish this program and you're walking at a fast pace for 25 minutes, uninterrupted, that puts you well on your way to finishing a 5-K. In 25 minutes, at 15 minutes per mile pace, you'll get 1.67 miles—in other words, more than halfway to a 5-K.

Whenever you find yourself ready to enter an event, the Stage 11 workouts on the facing page will help you prepare. The speed walk workout is 32 minutes—the longest of the program. If you complete all five workouts in a week, you'll be walking for 2 hours 43 minutes, a far cry from where you first started. Get through this stage, and the next one will feel easy.

Between the two speed walks and the one challenge walk, the Stage 11 workouts incorporate 65 minutes of total fast walking time. Remember, you can get an estimate of your speed by counting your steps for 1 minute. Look at the chart in Chapter 5 for a reminder of how steps-per-minute translate to speed.

By now, you might start feeling like you're maxing out at your top speed. You don't feel like your legs can move any faster. If that's the case, try out this next Technique Tip (page 212). It's more of an exercise, something to do during the warm-up portion of your walk.

The point of this exercise is to loosen up the hips. Looser hips will help you kick your speed up a notch.

But understand this: You would never want to have your feet cross over the imaginary center line during the fast walking. Why? It's

WALK YOUR BUTT OFF!

STAGE *11*

Minimum: 5 walks
Strength workouts*: 2–3 times this week

2 TO 4 BRISK WALKS

After warming up by walking at an easy pace for 2 to 3 minutes, you should walk at a purposeful pace, as if you need to get to an appointment, about 3 to 4 mph, for 30 to 40 minutes. Do a minimum of 2 brisk walks this week; a maximum of 4 if you're trying to walk every day.

Total workout time: 32–43 minutes

2 SPEED WALKS

➤ Start with a 2-minute warm-up at an easy pace.

➤ Then do 1 minute at a brisk pace, 15 minutes at a fast pace, 1 minute at a brisk pace, 10 minutes at a fast pace.

➤ End with 3 minutes of easy walking.

Total fast walking time: 25 minutes
Total workout time: 32 minutes

1 CHALLENGE WALK

➤ Start with a 5-minute warm-up (2 minutes easy, 3 minutes brisk).

➤ Then do 15 minutes as fast as you can, noting your starting point and finishing point or distance.

➤ Return and walk back to the start at a more comfortable pace.

Total workout time: At least 35 minutes

For the strength workout, see page 75.

Loosen up your hips

When you feel like you're walking so fast that you want to run, it's time to get your hips in on the action. Unfortunately, many of us have tight hips from too much sitting, so this week we're going to get them moving a little. During your warm-ups, try the "supermodel walk." Imagine there is a line between your feet. When you walk normally, your feet should be on either side of the line. But for this exercise, you want each foot to just cross over the line so you feel your hips moving more. Try it for just 30 to 60 seconds at a time. If you have lower-back problems, this may aggravate them, so proceed with caution and stop if you notice any discomfort.

wasted energy to move your foot across your body like that. When you're trying to walk fast, you want your legs going straight ahead of you, not across. This is just a limbering-up exercise. Try it in small doses during times you're walking at an easy pace.

Once you've spent a few walks focusing on Tip #10, here's another tip for your hips.

These tips are advanced-level techniques for maximizing your speed. You might find that the hip swivel slows you down the first few times you try it, but persevere. It takes awhile to get used to the hip action, but if you can master it, your speed will improve over time. And it gives your mind something to focus on during those long bouts of fast walking.

THE BIG PICTURE

If you've followed the program stage by stage, with no stops or stage repeats, you're 11 weeks in and on the verge of the final stage in the next chapter. Great job! By now, your exercise log reveals some impressive tallies: at least 55 exercise sessions, filling up most days of the week.

If that consistency has eluded you, no problem. Backtrack a little and aim for regularity ahead of speed and intensity. It's never too late to get in the habit and establish that firm routine of 5 days of exercise per week. You want to make exercise automatic, something you do most of your days for the rest of your life. Better to walk more days each week, even if it's at a slower pace, than to walk a few days really intensely. Consistency week in and week out will help you drop pounds and get faster over time. A few days of intense workouts followed by days off because you're sore or discouraged won't help you meet your goals.

TECHNIQUE TIP # 11

Swivel your hips

Now that your hips are loosened up (from practicing the supermodel walk), add a little swivel to help you go faster. Your hips should be moving forward and backward, not side to side like you're on a dance floor. Think of your legs extending all the way up to your belly button. This is not just an imaginative exercise. Some of your walking muscles do, in fact, go up into your abdomen. As your right leg steps forward, your right hip should sway forward. Then that right hip should sway back as your right leg extends behind you. Pull your belly button in and feel your ab muscles work as you swivel your hips.

This forward-and-back hip swivel is not a big movement. Warm up first with the supermodel walk, then practice the hip swivel for a minute or so. Intersperse a few minutes of focused hip swiveling into your walks, but don't spend all your time on it. Over time, it will start to click and become more natural.

FOOD TALK:
CRAVINGS

By now, you've kept at least two food logs during Stages 1 and 6. (Look out—we're going to ask you to keep one more.) You've thought about your breakfast, lunch, dinner, and snacks; how you time your meals; how fast you eat; where you eat; and what you eat.

So, what's left?

Cravings. Right. Those food hankerings that surprise us, hitting when we're least able to resist them. In fact, maybe that's how we should define a craving: the food you want to eat in a moment of weakness.

Leslie's advice about cravings might seem a bit unusual, but by now, you can probably guess what her philosophy is: You should have what it is you're after instead of denying yourself. Satisfy your craving.

But you can do that in a controlled way. Here's how:

Step 1

First, take a few minutes to think about and identify what it is you *really* desire. Not just the taste but the texture and temperature that you're after, too. Is it crunchy, creamy, sweet, or savory? Warm or cold?

Leslie puts it this way: "The most important thing about identifying the craving is that you don't stand in front of the refrigerator putting everything aimlessly into your mouth because you're trying to avoid what you really want. Or you're thinking, 'Let me look in the refrigerator and see what jumps out at me.' Well, everything does. So you eat five items and several hundred calories before finally getting to what it is you want."

Uh-Oh; I Fell Off the Wagon

So you've been sick, busy, or generally unmotivated, but now you're ready to get back out there. Great! Do yourself a favor, though, and don't try to pick up exactly where you left off. It's fine to go back a few stages and start rebuilding at an easier point. Don't get frustrated and burned out by trying to resume the routine at a challenging level. Remember, you're doing this for you.

Coach Michele offers this guideline: Go back one stage for each week you've missed. For 2 missed weeks, go back two stages. If you feel good at that stage, you can progress more quickly. Try a speed walk and a brisk walk during the next few days to see how they go. If they go well, you can bump up to the next stage on your next scheduled speed walk.

Step 2

When you've figured out what you really want, have some. Be mindful of your quantity. You don't have to eat a lot to satisfy a craving. Set the parameters and go get it. If it's ice cream you're after, buy a kiddie cone. If it's chips, go to the mini-mart and get a single-serving bag. Keeping a full-size bag at home invites overdoing it. Most people aren't disciplined enough to count out the 12 chips of a serving size and put the rest away.

Step 3

Be done. And acknowledge what you've just done. "I had a craving for chocolate, I ate two Dove chocolate squares, I'm done, and I feel better now."

With this strategy, you should be able to handle the strongest food desires. But be aware of how your environment plays a role. You might notice that you have cravings when you finish a stressful stint at work.

Or when you've finally gotten the kids to bed and the house is quiet and you're a little bored. Cravings intensify when we have things staring us in the face. You probably don't crave cake unless you know there's leftover birthday cake in the kitchen. Then your mind and gut tell you, yes, you're craving cake.

Before you indulge every craving, ask yourself if you can modify your environment to reduce the cravings. Walk immediately after your Thursday afternoon meeting. Cut a bowl of strawberries in the afternoon to eat in the evening in front of the TV. Clear out postparty leftovers, especially the half-eaten baked goods and the foods that didn't taste so good the first time you had them.

Some people swear it works to make yourself wait 10 minutes to see if you still *really* want that food before you have it.

And you know what? It's fine if you do. If you're in the mode of constantly denying yourself, then that can blow up into a much more damaging binge when you can't say no any longer.

Leslie advises making lists of appropriate foods for the problem times or when cravings hit. Write down what choices you have to eat and tape the list inside a cupboard. "I really like the idea of having lists," she says. "It takes the guesswork out or when you open up the refrigerator and everything is calling your name."

These are just examples. You can make your own list.

MY ANGER MANAGEMENT FOODS (CRUNCHY):

- 1-ounce package of whole wheat crackers
- 3 cups of air-popped popcorn
- 1 serving of pretzels
- Baby carrots with 2 tablespoons of hummus
- An apple with peanut butter
- 1 serving of pistachios in the shell

MY "I'M UPSET" FOODS (CREAMY):

- Honey vanilla Greek yogurt
- An individual pudding cup

MY COMFORT FOODS (WARM):

- Chicken noodle soup
- Skim milk latte

MY HAPPY FOODS (SWEET):

- 1 small muffin, the size of a tennis ball
- An apple, pear, or banana with 2 tablespoons of chocolate syrup for dipping
- 1 Skinny Cow cone or Hoodsie Cup of ice cream

Whatever you select, put it on a plate, get out the appropriate utensils, sit down at a table, and enjoy. Focus on the food, the flavor, the texture, and how you're feeling. Then be done.

THE LAST FOOD LOG

As we near the end of the Walk Your Butt Off! program, please take a few days to keep a final food log. As you did during Stages 1 and 6, 3 days of logging (or longer if you want) is optimal. Include everything you eat, and if it works out, keep track of your intake on a weekend day. We're including a template at the end of the book (pages 274–277).

There are two new questions on the log, to reflect what you've learned. This time, record tallies for your protein and fiber, topics we covered in Chapters 6 and 10. You don't have to do those calculations at the moment you eat the food—you can go back and look it up later—but this forces you to reckon with how you're doing in those important categories.

On the next page, we'll show you Charlene Nelson's food log for one day at the end of the program.

WALK YOUR BUTT OFF! *Food Log*

TIME:	WHAT YOU ATE AND THE AMOUNT:	WHAT YOU DRANK:	WHERE WERE YOU?	WERE YOU HUNGRY? Y/N	P (G)	F (G)
7:30 a.m.	Scrambled egg whites with spinach and sunflower seeds 5 med. egg whites, ⅓ cup spinach, 2 Tbsp sunflower seeds	Hot apple cider	Kitchen table	Y	17 g	6 g
10:00 a.m.	1 Tbsp peanut butter, 8 celery sticks			Y	5.6 g	2.6 g
1:00 p.m.	Rainbow broccoli slaw (color!!!) topped with 5 oz boiled shrimp 1 cup slaw	Water with lemon	Kitchen table	Y	30.8 g	5 g
7:00 p.m.	Boneless pork ribs and sauerkraut, apple and onion, caraway seeds in the slow cooker (YUM) with mashed sweet potatoes (color!!!)	Water with lemon	Kitchen table	Y	21 g	9 g

Contrast what Charlene was eating at the end of the program with what she was eating in Stage 1:

WALK YOUR BUTT OFF! *Food Log*

TIME:	WHAT YOU ATE:	WHAT YOU DRANK:	WHERE:
7:00 a.m.	1 small banana	Water	Kitchen
8:00 a.m.	1 slice of Wegmans Marathon Bread toasted with 1 Tbsp raspberry preserves	Water	Family room
11:30 a.m.	16 white corn lime-flavored tortilla chips; 1 Greek raspberry yogurt	Water	Den
5:00 p.m.	1 can lentil soup	Water	Kitchen
8:00 p.m.	6–8 mini Tootsie Rolls	Water	At the parade

Charlene wasn't a terrible eater at the beginning. Greek yogurt gave her protein, as did the lentil soup, which provided a healthy wallop of fiber, too. But her day was quite pale. Banana, chips, toast, yogurt. They lack color.

Fast-forward 12 weeks, and Leslie was thrilled by Charlene's progress: "She's getting substantial protein at every meal," Leslie points out. "She's eating a much wider variety of foods. The color at every meal is impressive. And she's going the extra mile to quantify it, which shows that she has really learned about the food she's eating." (Clearly, Charlene had done her homework to figure out that her celery sticks and peanut butter have 2.6 grams of fiber.)

She is also paying attention to her internal cues, whether she's hungry or not, and not just focusing on what's on the plate in front of her or eating just because it's dinnertime. In short, "Charlene is healthing it up, coloring it up, muscling it up," according to Leslie. Bravo.

This is a win for Charlene. And it will be for you, too, if you take the time to keep track and then look at your log.

WHAT DID YOU LEARN?

Filling out this log in its entirety shows how much you've learned. You're a more educated eater. You know more about your habits now than when you started because you can keep an accurate record of your quantities of food, fiber, and protein, and your level of hunger. But what's most important is this: *You* look at it. In fact, bring out your first log from Week 1. Compare and contrast your first and final logs. What do you notice? What has changed? What are you proud of? What still needs work?

Remember the guiding principles behind the nutrition advice that Leslie offered in Chapter 1? Here they are again. See where you fit in with these now.

1. **There are no quick fixes.** You could eliminate all carbohydrates from your diet for a few weeks, and you'll probably shed some pounds. The better move, however, is developing habits that are sustainable for life. Otherwise, the weight goes right back on. Diets fail because they're for a fixed time period, and when the diet ends, the pounds creep back.

2. **All-or-nothing plans are a recipe for failure.** You might resolve to give up all sugar and fat and shop exclusively at the farmers' market. Rather than attempting a sudden, radical shift in your habits—a change that will be hard to maintain—try a step-by-step

approach to overhauling your eating by improving your choices one meal at a time. Prepare to bargain with yourself, compromise, and make trade-offs rather than holding yourself to an impossible set of standards.

3. **Losing weight is about more than just what you eat.** It's also about when, where, how much, why, and even with whom you eat.

4. **Solutions have to fit your life.** If you don't have time to cook, you can't be expected to follow intricate recipes. You need to develop a plan to eat well in the time you have. If that includes dinner at a Subway once a week or canned soup and a tuna sandwich for dinner, there's nothing wrong with that.

Take this time to figure out what you've done differently during these past 12 weeks that has helped you. What can you carry forward? What is sustainable? Are there some things you tried that just didn't work for you at all? It's important to acknowledge that, too. If there's something new you want to try to work on next, make a note of that. Here's a place where you can puzzle it out. You can also use page 279 in the workbook.

Since I kept my first food log, the biggest changes to my eating have been _____

_____

I think I can continue these habits _____

_____

Next, I'd like to work on _____

_____

_____

_____

CHAPTER **11** # To-Do List

☐ Take a look at your calendar to plan at least five times you can walk during the next week.

☐ Complete at least five workouts, including at least 2 brisk walks, 2 speed walks, and your third 15-minute challenge walk. Don't schedule speed walks and/or challenge walks on back-to-back days. Make a note of how far you go during your challenge walk. Did you cover more ground than you did during the previous stage?

☐ Complete at least two sets of strength exercises on nonconsecutive days.

☐ Think about your cravings. When do you get them? Can you change your habits to minimize cravings? If you get a craving, how can you satisfy it in a controlled way?

☐ Keep one last food log and compare it to the one you did at the beginning of the program. How does it look now? What have you learned?

SECRETS
of the
TEST PANEL

Age: 55

Height: 5'4"

Total pounds lost:
13.2 *pounds*
in 12 weeks

Total inches lost:
2¼ *inches,*
**including 1 inch
from her waist and
2¼ inches from her hips**

Starting walk time:
18:50

Ending walk time:
15:51

Faster by:
2 minutes
59 seconds

Before

Gail Fragassi

Day job: I'm the director of a child care center, and some evenings I work at a Hallmark store. I've been married for 31 years.

How I got here: I used to love walking, but I didn't have the ambition to get going again. The biggest obstacle for me was getting out of my rut and making the time to exercise. Also, fullness was always hard for me. I never knew I was full until I was stuffed.

How I started: I followed the program, but I had trouble getting my speed much faster for the speed walks. So I adapted the program and kept it fairly steady, pushing to a fast pace for a few minutes at the end of workouts. I was pretty new to this kind of exercise, and I didn't want to overdo it too early. It has been a great learning experience for me. The program was exactly what I needed to get moving and feel better about myself.

Winning strategies: My biggest change has been increasing my protein and fiber. I'm making an effort to eat breakfast before work and I'm trying to plan ahead for the nights I go to my second job. The food over the holidays was very challenging, but I believe I came through it better than other years. I was able to limit my quantities and choices and still enjoy it. I made sure to get treats out of my office. I am glad that's all over now and I can go back to better food choices.

Fringe benefits: I notice going up the steps is easier at work. Even when I'm carrying loads of supplies and I need to make two trips, I always take the steps now. Sometimes when I couldn't fit in a workout on the days I was working both jobs, I would walk at lunch with my coworkers, anywhere from 15 to 30 minutes. It was nice to interact with them that way.

Secret weapon: I got a new blender, the Ninja, for making smoothies with Greek yogurt. It's great!

CHAPTER 12

60
Workouts
AND COUNTING

This is it.
The grand finale.
Time to close it out.

With this stage's workout, you'll reach the final goal: walking fast for 25 minutes straight.

Now, I know what you're thinking. The longest you've ever walked fast is 15 minutes in a row in the last stage's speed walk and with the recent challenge walks. So how are you expected to suddenly make the leap from 15 minutes fast to 25 minutes fast? Seems a little daunting, right?

Well, don't psych yourself out. The difference between the Stage 11 speed workout and this current workout is one measly minute. That's right. One. Remember, in Stage 11, the prescribed workout was 1 brisk, 15 fast, 1 brisk, 10 fast. Now you're just erasing that second minute of brisk walking. You can do this.

Find your toughest self. Stick to the workout. Don't fear it, and don't make excuses.

Give it your best try.

When you do the speed walk for the first time, be sure to make some extra notes in your walking log. You deserve some exclamation points or at least some editorial comments like "Wow! That was pretty cool. Didn't think I would be able to do that when I started this program."

You get the idea. You should celebrate your achievement.

While you're at it, pay special attention to the challenge walk, which will give you visible proof of how far you've come in the 12 stages of this book. Make sure you record your progress, and notice just how much farther you're able to walk than you were back at the start of the program.

WALK YOUR BUTT OFF!

STAGE *12*

Minimum: 5 walks
Strength workouts*: 2–3 times this week

2 TO 4 BRISK WALKS

After warming up by walking at an easy pace for 2 to 3 minutes, you should walk at a purposeful pace, as if you need to get to an appointment, about 3 to 4 mph, for 30 to 40 minutes. Do a minimum of 2 brisk walks this week; a maximum of 4 if you're trying to walk every day.

Total workout time: 32–43 minutes

2 SPEED WALKS

➤ Start with a 2-minute warm-up at an easy pace.

➤ Then do 1 minute at a brisk pace, 25 minutes at a fast pace.

➤ End with 3 minutes of easy walking.

Total fast walking time: 25 minutes.
Total workout time: 31 minutes.

1 CHALLENGE WALK

➤ Start with a 5-minute warm-up (2 minutes easy, 3 minutes brisk).

➤ Then do 15 minutes as fast as you can, noting your starting point and finishing point or distance.

➤ Return and walk back to the start at a more comfortable pace.

Total workout time: At least 35 minutes

For the strength workout, see page 75.

PRACTICE MAKES PERFECT

Your technique will continue to improve with time and practice, and better technique will lead to faster speeds. Faster speeds burn more calories, helping you lose weight, which in turn makes it easier to go faster. So don't neglect technique. Below, Michele shows you how to incorporate all the tips you've learned into your future walking career.

Over time, you'll find yourself naturally doing these things when you walk. Even when you check in on an area of the body—your elbows and back, your feet, your butt, your core—you won't need to make adjustments because you're doing it exactly right. But getting to the point where it feels automatic takes a lot of conscious effort. And remember, with these tweaks to your technique, walking fast is easier and feels smoother. Seeing progress in your speed will help keep you motivated and moving, striving to reach new goals.

TECHNIQUE TIP # 12

• Pull it all together

During one walk a week, pay extra attention to your technique. Practice the key moves below by focusing on each for a minute at a time. Repeat until you've done each for 3 minutes total. For a visual refresher, turn back to the posture diagram on page 30.

- Drive your elbows back and squeeze your shoulder blades. Remember to look forward, not at your feet.
- Roll from your heel to your toes, and push off with your toes.
- Squeeze your glutes each time your heel lands on the ground.
- Pull your belly button in and feel your ab muscles work as you swivel your hips.

The Walker's High

Do you get a "high" during or after exercise? A friend of mine, Vince, 53, has been running for years. I never knew he was a walker. But he had this to say about exercise-induced euphoria:

"I walk as often as possible and do a 3-mile walk at least once a week. I walk a 15-minute mile, which isn't all that much slower than what I run, which is about 10. But even though I've run a half-marathon and spent 3 months training for it with runs up to 10 miles, I have never experienced the so-called runner's high. I have, however, experienced this numerous times when walking, and it's extremely pleasant. I understand why it's addictive. Why do I get it when walking but not when running? My guess is that it's because I'm not as winded—at least not the way I get when I'm running. All I really know is that I like it a lot."

WHAT'S IN STORE?

Completing the 12-stage Walk Your Butt Off! program is a huge accomplishment. Acknowledge it and treat yourself to a reward like a new pair of walking shoes, an upgrade on your watch, or a high-end jacket or shirt that you can use for speed walks.

Then ask yourself: What's next?

"It's important to set a new goal," Coach Michele says. "What are you going to do next with your fitter, healthier body?"

Maybe you want to try a new activity like Zumba or Pilates. Perhaps you'll sign up for a 5-K, 10-K, or a half-marathon walking event. Or look around for an active vacation like a cycling trip through Napa or a walking vacation in the Swiss Alps.

Of course, no matter what athletic endeavors you might pursue, you'll always have walking. No matter where you find yourself, as long as you have a good pair of sneakers, you can go out for 30 minutes and get a solid workout. Even if it's snowing heavily and all you can find is one plowed parking lot, that will do. You can always walk. Don't forget that.

Choose a new goal that will motivate you to stick to all the healthy habits you've been developing over the past 3 months. Spend some walking time mulling it over.

We'll leave a few lines here for you to write down your next fitness goals. Where do you see yourself?

Within 1 month, I will _____

Within 6 months, I will _____

This time next year, I will _____

Do you have a weight goal, too? With about 9 or 10 miles of walking each week, requiring about $2\frac{1}{2}$ hours of your time, you're much healthier than you were when you started. And health and vitality are the most important things you can give yourself, with or without weight loss.

It is our hope—and the experience of the test panelists—that all this walking and nutrition advice has helped you shed some pounds. And it's natural to want to keep losing more. Take a moment to state your next weight loss goal here. (Be realistic. By now you know how much weight you were able to lose in 12 weeks. Do you think you can keep up that rate of change?)

I would like to lose _____ pounds in the next 3 months.

YOUR NEXT STEPS

Our test panelists expressed three recurring themes when we asked them about their next goals.

- Many wanted to walk longer—not necessarily an ultrawalk like Gayle Hendricks's 50-K, but a 10-K or a half-marathon.
- A few of them were curious about trying running.
- Several said they wanted to lose 5, 10, or 20 additional pounds.

Coach Michele and I put our heads together to help them get started. Here's what we sent them for the next steps.

GOAL: TRAIN FOR A 10-K EVENT (6.2 MILES)

Training for an event that's beyond your current abilities is a great way to stay motivated and keep walking interesting. Recruit some friends and family members to join you to make the training and the event more fun. And you don't have to be at your goal weight to do it. In fact, the event might help you get to your goal weight.

If this is your first 10-K or if it has been more than a year since you did a walk of that length, your goal is to simply finish the 6.2 miles. Don't worry about hitting a certain time—that's for the future.

You'll need at least 6 full weeks to train for it properly. Here's how:

Your 10-K Training Plan

Continue using Stage 12 from the Walk Your Butt Off! program as the basis of your routine. You will **replace the challenge walk with long walks**, as outlined on the following page.

LONG WALKS

The goal of these workouts is to build your distance and duration, not speed. In other words, these long walks get you used to spending an extended period of time on your feet and moving. Remember to stretch afterward by using the moves outlined in Chapter 3.

WEEKS	DURATION	SPECIAL INSTRUCTIONS
1	45 minutes	Walk for 45 minutes at a moderate intensity. Remember to warm up first and cool down at the end for all your long walks.
2	60 minutes	Walk for 60 minutes at a moderate intensity.

This is a perfect time to sign up for and walk a 5-K (3.1 miles) so you're familiar with the race experience before doing a longer event.

3	60 minutes	Walk at a moderate intensity for 4 miles. If you complete this in less than 60 minutes, you can continue walking to finish up the hour.
4	varies	Walk at a moderate intensity for 5 miles.
5	varies	Walk at a moderate intensity for 6 miles.
6	varies	Now you're ready to do a 10-K. In the week leading up to the event, stick to brisk walks and keep them to 45 minutes or less. This will allow your body the rest and recovery it needs to be strong on race day. **End of week: Race**

SAMPLE SCHEDULE						
Day 1	Day 2	Day 3	Day 4	Day 5	Day 6	Day 7
Speed walk 31 minutes	Brisk walk 30–40 minutes	Speed walk 31 minutes	Strength workout	Long walk 45+ minutes	Strength workout	Brisk walk 30–40 minutes

You'll see the pattern: Add a mile each week to your long walk to get ready to go the distance. If it's a half-marathon you're planning, continue adding one long walk per week, increasing the distance of the long walk 1 mile at a time up to 11 miles. (It's fine to stop a little short of your goal distance and save it for race day.) Also, every fourth or fifth week, give yourself a break and return to 6 miles for the long walk.

GOAL: GIVE RUNNING A TRY

Running might seem like the natural next step after you feel like you've mastered walking. But you use your muscles in different ways when running. Also, running puts greater force on your joints. With walking, one foot is on the ground at all times. Not true of running. When you break into a run, you get momentarily airborne. During each stride, there's a moment when both feet are off the ground. In a sense, you're jumping from foot to foot. Being off the ground, however, requires you to land with a lot more force than if you're walking. That's frequently the cause of injuries to runners—the impact on feet, shins, knees, and backs.

Pssst! Here's the Secret of Beginner Running

That doesn't mean every runner gets injured. Not at all. You just have to be smart about it: Run slowly, increase your distance gradually, and listen to your body.

In 2010, I worked with 30 new runners for *Run Your Butt Off!*, my first book. The coach for that group, Budd Coates, had been an elite runner in his twenties and thirties, and he qualified for the US Olympic marathon trials four times.

Still, it was his instruction that helped that group of test panelists achieve their goal: a 30-minute nonstop run.

What's the secret?

Run slow. Run no faster than your fast walk, especially in the first 6 weeks of running.

If you try to run faster than you're ready for, you'll find yourself huffing and puffing, out of breath at the side of the road or the trail, and feeling miserable. So go slow enough that you're not totally winded. You'll be more likely to stick with it. Don't worry about speed at first; just aim for consistency.

The first stage of the Run Your Butt Off! program is easy enough for you: Build up to 30 minutes of nonstop walking. You can do that already.

Here's the Stage 2 workout:

RUN YOUR BUTT OFF!

STAGE 2

➤ Walk for 4 minutes. Run for 1 minute.
➤ Repeat the sequence four more times.
➤ End with 4 minutes of walking.

**Total workout time: 29 minutes,
5 of which are running**

Do this workout at least three or four times
in a week before moving on to the next stage.

If you're paying attention, you'll notice that this workout appears very similar to the beginning of the Walk Your Butt Off! program. The philosophy is the same: Gradually build up. Don't shock your body. Be nice to yourself and exercise consistently, and you'll make huge improvements in just 12 weeks.

Here's the Stage 3 running program. But after that, you'll have to check out the book to see what comes next!

RUN YOUR BUTT OFF!

STAGE 3

➤ Walk for 4 minutes. Run for 2 minutes.
➤ Repeat the sequence four more times.
➤ End with 3 minutes of walking.

Total workout time: 33 minutes, 10 of which are running

Do this workout at least three or four times in a week before moving on to the next stage.

In just two stages, you'll double the amount of running you're doing. Remember: Slow is key.

GOAL: LOSE MORE WEIGHT

Are you happy where you are with your walking but not happy with what the scale says? Here's Coach Michele's take on it: "You need to continue to challenge your body to keep on shedding pounds," she says. "If you do the same workouts over and over, your body becomes accustomed to them and doesn't have to work as hard, so you burn fewer calories."

In addition, as you shrink in size, you burn fewer calories doing the same activities you did when you weighed more. Think about it: It takes more effort (calorie burn) to move a 200-pound body for a mile than it does to move a 160-pound body for a mile.

All this makes taking off those final stubborn pounds harder and sets you up for the dreaded plateau—when the scale just won't budge. So if you still have pounds to lose, the long walk program and the running program will probably help jolt your body into relinquishing some pounds. But if those don't interest you, try intervals.

For one thing, you will be burning as many calories as you would from doing a regular walk but you would do so in half the time. Even if you lightened up over the last 12 weeks, pushing your body to walk intervals could be the fat-burning boost you need to break your

Your 10-K Training Plan

Continue using Stage 12 from the Walk Your Butt Off! program as the basis of your routine. You will **replace the challenge walk with interval walks,** as outlined on the following pages.

plateau. Take this well-regarded study from the University of New South Wales: Researchers divided 45 women in their twenties and at a healthy weight into two groups. Half the women pedaled a stationary bike at a moderate intensity for 40 minutes while the other group of women cycled for 20 minutes with intervals of speeding up for 8 seconds and slowing down for 12 seconds. The 20-minute cyclers burned about as many calories as the 40-minute cyclers—200 calories in half the time!

If that sounds good to you, check out Michele's program here.

These interval walks, when you reach your top speed, require a short burst of effort at that level, followed by a recovery time. Alternating between the fast walking and the easy recovery will challenge your body in new ways—and keep the pounds coming off. For more information, see Michele's book, *Walk Off Weight*. For fresh walking ideas, event-training advice, and other fitness inspiration, you can also visit Michele's site, mywalkingcoach.com.

INTERVAL WALKS

- Start with a 2-minute warm-up at an easy pace, then gradually build to a brisk pace for 3 minutes.

- Go as fast as you can for 15 seconds. Push yourself to a very hard intensity, to the point where you're breathing so hard, you can only speak one word at a time.

- Recover for 45 seconds, walking at an easy pace.

- Repeat this pattern of 15 seconds hard/45 seconds easy for 15 to 20 minutes.

- End with 5 minutes of easy walking.

Total workout time: 25 to 30 minutes

You're starting out with a ratio of 15 seconds at top speed to 45 seconds of recovery. This ratio will change as you progress through the program. See Coach Michele's schedule below:

WEEKS	SPECIAL INSTRUCTIONS
13–16	Repeat Week 12 from the main program.
17–20	Replace the challenge walk with an interval walk. All other workouts are similar to Week 12. Here's a sample schedule:

SAMPLE SCHEDULE						
Day 1	Day 2	Day 3	Day 4	Day 5	Day 6	Day 7
Speed walk 31 minutes	Brisk walk 30–40 minutes	Speed walk 31 minutes	Strength workout	Interval walk 30 minutes	Strength workout	Brisk walk 30–40 minutes

WEEKS	SPECIAL INSTRUCTIONS
21–24	Repeat Week 20 with a more challenging interval walk. Do 20-second vigorous intervals with 40-second recovery intervals.
25–28	Repeat Week 20 with a more challenging interval walk. Do 30-second vigorous intervals with 30-second recovery intervals.
29 AND BEYOND	If you'd like to lose more weight, continue alternating Week 12 workouts with Week 28 workouts. Do each for 4 to 6 weeks, then switch. This will help challenge your body so you continue to see results.

MILESTONES

One of our test panelists likes to count miles. Midway through the program, Bill Kealey informed me that he had covered 110 miles. (He was walking to and from work every day, and he was fast.) He loves keeping track of the distance. It's more satisfying for him than stepping on the scale, an impressive measure of how far he has come.

Kristen Tomasic checks her Fitbit, and on a really sedentary day in the office, she'll invite a colleague for a walking meeting.

Val Donohue likes to count her steps per minute and continually push herself to walk a little faster, aiming to increase her pace by at least one more step each minute she checks.

Lorraine Wiedorn was set on getting back to doing what she calls "men's pushups" on the floor. She's doing them now. Will she get to the 50 she could do 20 years ago?

Gayle Hendricks keeps challenging herself to enter walking and stairclimbing events. Every month, I get another e-mail from her describing an event she has signed up for.

They're all looking forward, knowing they'll improve themselves in the future. That's what we love to hear.

You are now a body of work: Your body reflects the work you've put in. You're healthier, faster, stronger, and leaner. You've put in 60 workouts; and I hope you have a record of them somewhere because the visual impact of 60 workouts, either on paper or on screen, is quite impressive.

Please use the resources on the following pages to help you chart your course in the future. Whatever reinforcement you need to keep going, find it and use it. It would be a shame to finish 60 walks and then return to sedentary ways. Think about something or someone—like Bill, Kristen, Val, Lorraine, or Gayle—who motivates you, and keep at it.

Remember, on the days that you don't feel like doing any walking, even a little is better than none. You can't go a full 30 minutes? Go for 20. Can't go 20? Go for 15 or 10 or whatever you can muster.

Coach Michele Stanten, dietitian Leslie Bonci, and I are all rooting for you. Our hope for you is that this is just the beginning of a life of activity, walking, and healthier eating habits. We love to hear stories from people who lose weight, get faster, finish races, have more energy, and plain feel better.

So please keep up the good work. Your life depends on it.

To-Do List

☐ Take a look at your calendar to plan at least five times you can walk during the next week.

☐ Complete at least five workouts, including at least 2 brisk walks, 2 speed walks, and your final 15-minute challenge walk. Don't schedule speed walks and/or challenge walks on back-to-back days. Make a note of how far you go during your challenge walk. Did you cover more ground than you did during the previous stage?

☐ Complete at least two sets of strength exercises on nonconsecutive days.

☐ Now that you've finished the Walk Your Butt Off! program, what is your next goal?

☐ Do another 1-mile walk test (see instructions on page 10). Don't forget to write your new time in the workbook on page 244!

Age: 45

Height: 5'4"

Total pounds lost:
6 pounds
in 12 weeks

Total inches lost:
2½ inches,
including 1½ inches
from her hips

Starting walk time:
15:40

Ending walk time:
12:15

Faster by:
3 minutes
25 seconds

Before

Deb Davies

Day job: I'm a reading coach. I'm married with two daughters.

How I got here: Before I had my first daughter, who is 11, I weighed 135. I got up as high as 172 about 4 years ago. When I was working on my doctorate, I kept really weird hours. I would often work in the middle of the night, adding a fourth meal to keep me awake. Since then, I've always paid attention to what I eat. But my metabolism is minimal. It's hard for me to lose weight.

Winning strategies: I'm really focused on protein. I've added in cottage cheese to my yogurt for breakfast every morning. I'll add canned chicken to soup. I've discovered edamame as a snack. With a big glass of water, it really fills you up. My daughters are packing more protein in their school lunches, too.

Workout mind-set: I walk some outside and a lot more on the treadmill than I used to. I feel like the speed walks are the most important ones for weight loss, but I've had to learn it's better to get through the whole workout than to kill yourself on the first speed interval!

Accountability is key: The program, and having to send in my logs, has been important. On Thanksgiving Day, I had to get up at 6 a.m. to get a walk in before we left for the day. I never would have done that before. Having people watch what you're doing changes your mind-set. I'm looking for ways to replicate that accountability when the program ends, such as joining an online fitness community.

Best advice: It's not realistic to go through the holidays and deprive yourself completely. Make little changes, changes that can last. The results might not be drastic, but they'll stick.

WALK YOUR BUTT OFF!
Workbook

YOU'LL HAVE A BETTER SHOT AT ACCOMPLISHING YOUR GOALS IF YOU WRITE DOWN WHAT YOU'RE DOING.

That's the truth. Years of scientific study—and powerful anecdotal evidence from these authors' lives—have shown that if you make a record of your activity and your eating, you'll be more likely to succeed.

In the following pages, we present to you a Walk Your Butt Off! workbook, a place where you can write down your workouts, including the places you walk and your thoughts on how walking feels, on a week-by-week basis.

In select places, we insert food logs, places for you to write down what you're eating for 2 or 3 days at a time. You don't have to do it every week. (That would get tedious.) But a periodic checkup on your meals and on those unexpected bites between meals can give you the reality check you need to stick to your eating plan. An unflinching look at what you're consuming can help you make the changes you want to make.

Each week, we also present "Food for Thought," a probing question or bit of advice for you to chew on. The questions are meant to help you think, examine your habits, and understand what's holding you back or helping you succeed.

Rest assured, no one has to see this. It's for your eyes only. It's meant to be a tool to help you, to motivate you, to encourage you. The hope is that as you compare your workouts from the beginning of the program to the end, you'll delight in your accomplishments—and be motivated to keep setting the bar higher for yourself.

Whatever your health goals may be, we want you to enjoy the Walk Your Butt Off! journey. And we hope this workbook makes the path a little easier.

A note about the scale: Try to weigh yourself at the same time of day, ideally in the morning. Wake up, use the bathroom, take off your clothes, step on the scale. And then be done with the scale for another week. Many people who are trying to shed pounds weigh themselves every day—or sometimes several times during the course of the day. Our body weight fluctuates depending on so many factors, like water consumption, recent meals, and the clothes we're wearing. It's pointless to check the scale too often. It can be discouraging, too. Find a consistent schedule for weighing yourself that you're happy with, but it should never be more than once a day. We think once a week is perfect.

In Chapter 1, we discuss how to test yourself walking a mile. Use the space below to write down your 1-mile walk time.

DATE	MY 1-MILE WALK TIME	:

(minutes) (seconds)

In Chapter 1, we also discuss how you can predict your walk time after completing the program. Fill in your predicted 1-mile walk time in 12 weeks here:

PREDICTED DATE	MY PREDICTED 1-MILE WALK TIME	:

(minutes) (seconds)

Once you complete all 12 weeks, it will be time to do another walk test! Come back to this page once you have finished Stage 12 and write down your latest walk time to compare to your prediction. How did you do?

DATE	MY 1-MILE WALK TIME	:

(minutes) (seconds)

YOUR WORKOUT LOG

For each stage, we give you a workout log, starting on page 246. Just record the walking workouts you're doing and any additional activity. A workout log is great for many reasons. It helps you keep track of your workouts, and in so doing, you'll see improvements. And success begets success. Seeing your progress on paper will give you a boost to keep going!

STAGE 1 *Workout Log*

DATE	4/2	COURSE: Jasper Park trail

WORKOUT TIME/TYPE: Speed walk: 2 warm-up, 4 brisk, 1 fast, repeated 4 times, 3 cooldown   Total minutes: 25

NOTES (INCLUDE HOW YOU FELT, WEATHER, ETC.): Chilly wind; felt better after 15 minutes of walking	ADDITIONAL ACTIVITY: Yoga class; walked the dogs after dinner

YOUR FOOD LOG

During stages 1, 6, and 10, we'll give you a few pages to keep a food log. It's a 3-day record of what you eat. Every bite. Your food log will be more complete if you include a weekend day. (Many people tend to eat differently on the weekends than they do during the workweek.) None of us know what we eat unless we log it. Sometimes, it's not the meals that are the problem. It's all the "in betweens" that can mean the difference between a healthy weight and extra pounds. It all adds up. But you need to log it to see that. Here's a sample:

WALK YOUR BUTT OFF! *Food Log*

DATE	April 25			
TIME:	**WHAT YOU ATE:**	**WHAT YOU DRANK:**	**WHERE:**	
6:15 a.m.	¾ cup Cheerios with 2% milk and 1 teaspoon sugar; whole banana	Water	Home	
9:00 a.m.	6 baby carrots, 6 sugar peas, 1 ounce local sharp Cheddar	Water	Job 1	
12:15 p.m.	¼ (whole 8-inch) focaccia sandwich with turkey, salsa, Cheddar; 20 french fries; 2 slices dill pickle	16-ounce Dr Pepper	Job 1, cafeteria	
4:30 p.m.	3 ounces pan-fried beef coated with egg and bread crumbs; leftover egg; about 4 small turnips, mashed, with 1 tablespoon butter	Water	Home (This is really too close to lunch, but I work till 10 p.m. I don't want to eat then.)	

STAGE 1 *Workout Log*

DATE	COURSE:

WORKOUT TIME/TYPE:

NOTES (include how you felt, weather, etc.): | **ADDITIONAL ACTIVITY:**

DATE	COURSE:

WORKOUT TIME/TYPE:

NOTES (include how you felt, weather, etc.): | **ADDITIONAL ACTIVITY:**

DATE	COURSE:

WORKOUT TIME/TYPE:

NOTES (include how you felt, weather, etc.): | **ADDITIONAL ACTIVITY:**

DATE	COURSE:

WORKOUT TIME/TYPE:

NOTES (include how you felt, weather, etc.): | **ADDITIONAL ACTIVITY:**

DATE	COURSE:

WORKOUT TIME/TYPE:

NOTES (include how you felt, weather, etc.): | **ADDITIONAL ACTIVITY:**

DATE	COURSE:	
WORKOUT TIME/TYPE:		
NOTES (include how you felt, weather, etc.):	**ADDITIONAL ACTIVITY:**	

DATE	COURSE:	
WORKOUT TIME/TYPE:		
NOTES (include how you felt, weather, etc.):	**ADDITIONAL ACTIVITY:**	

TOTAL WORKOUTS FOR THE WEEK:	TOTAL WALKING MINUTES FOR THE WEEK:

FOOD LOG #1

On the next few pages, log your meals over at least 3 days this week, including a weekend day. Be sure to note the times you eat so you can see how long you are waiting between meals. Try to record *everything*, even that handful of almonds or the sleeve of Oreos. Also write down where you were when you were eating. Remember, the more honest you are, the more likely you will be to identify patterns that may be hindering your weight loss.

WALK YOUR BUTT OFF! *Food Log*

TIME:	WHAT YOU ATE:	WHAT YOU DRANK:	WHERE:

WALK YOUR BUTT OFF! *Food Log*

TIME:	WHAT YOU ATE:	WHAT YOU DRANK:	WHERE:

WALK YOUR BUTT OFF! *Food Log*

TIME:	WHAT YOU ATE:	WHAT YOU DRANK:	WHERE:

WALK YOUR BUTT OFF! *Food Log*

DATE				
TIME:	WHAT YOU ATE:		WHAT YOU DRANK:	WHERE:

WEIGHT THIS WEEK

STAGE 2 *Workout Log*

DATE	COURSE:

WORKOUT TIME/TYPE:

NOTES (include how you felt, weather, etc.): | ADDITIONAL ACTIVITY:

DATE	COURSE:

WORKOUT TIME/TYPE:

NOTES (include how you felt, weather, etc.): | ADDITIONAL ACTIVITY:

DATE	COURSE:

WORKOUT TIME/TYPE:

NOTES (include how you felt, weather, etc.): | ADDITIONAL ACTIVITY:

DATE	COURSE:

WORKOUT TIME/TYPE:

NOTES (include how you felt, weather, etc.): | ADDITIONAL ACTIVITY:

DATE	COURSE:

WORKOUT TIME/TYPE:

NOTES (include how you felt, weather, etc.): | ADDITIONAL ACTIVITY:

DATE	COURSE:

WORKOUT TIME/TYPE:

NOTES (include how you felt, weather, etc.):	ADDITIONAL ACTIVITY:

DATE	COURSE:

WORKOUT TIME/TYPE:

NOTES (include how you felt, weather, etc.):	ADDITIONAL ACTIVITY:

TOTAL WORKOUTS FOR THE WEEK:	TOTAL WALKING MINUTES FOR THE WEEK:

FOOD FOR THOUGHT

Look back at your food log from last week and think about how you've been eating. What are your biggest dietary challenges? If you could change one thing about your eating, what would it be?

STAGE 3 *Workout Log*

DATE | COURSE:

WORKOUT TIME/TYPE:

NOTES (include how you felt, weather, etc.): | **ADDITIONAL ACTIVITY:**

DATE | COURSE:

WORKOUT TIME/TYPE:

NOTES (include how you felt, weather, etc.): | **ADDITIONAL ACTIVITY:**

DATE | COURSE:

WORKOUT TIME/TYPE:

NOTES (include how you felt, weather, etc.): | **ADDITIONAL ACTIVITY:**

DATE | COURSE:

WORKOUT TIME/TYPE:

NOTES (include how you felt, weather, etc.): | **ADDITIONAL ACTIVITY:**

DATE | COURSE:

WORKOUT TIME/TYPE:

NOTES (include how you felt, weather, etc.): | **ADDITIONAL ACTIVITY:**

DATE		COURSE:	
WORKOUT TIME/TYPE:			
NOTES (include how you felt, weather, etc.):		**ADDITIONAL ACTIVITY:**	

DATE		COURSE:	
WORKOUT TIME/TYPE:			
NOTES (include how you felt, weather, etc.):		**ADDITIONAL ACTIVITY:**	

TOTAL WORKOUTS FOR THE WEEK:	**TOTAL WALKING MINUTES FOR THE WEEK:**

FOOD FOR THOUGHT

Think about your most challenging mealtimes. Do you have trouble making time for a hearty, protein-packed breakfast? Maybe you skip lunches or find yourself getting take-out for dinner more often than you'd like. Write down your biggest mealtime challenge and two steps you can take to change that pattern.

STAGE 4 *Workout Log*

DATE | COURSE:

WORKOUT TIME/TYPE:

NOTES (include how you felt, weather, etc.): | ADDITIONAL ACTIVITY:

DATE | COURSE:

WORKOUT TIME/TYPE:

NOTES (include how you felt, weather, etc.): | ADDITIONAL ACTIVITY:

DATE | COURSE:

WORKOUT TIME/TYPE:

NOTES (include how you felt, weather, etc.): | ADDITIONAL ACTIVITY:

DATE | COURSE:

WORKOUT TIME/TYPE:

NOTES (include how you felt, weather, etc.): | ADDITIONAL ACTIVITY:

DATE | COURSE:

WORKOUT TIME/TYPE:

NOTES (include how you felt, weather, etc.): | ADDITIONAL ACTIVITY:

DATE		COURSE:

WORKOUT TIME/TYPE:

NOTES (include how you felt, weather, etc.):	ADDITIONAL ACTIVITY:

DATE		COURSE:

WORKOUT TIME/TYPE:

NOTES (include how you felt, weather, etc.):	ADDITIONAL ACTIVITY:

TOTAL WORKOUTS FOR THE WEEK:	TOTAL WALKING MINUTES FOR THE WEEK:

FOOD FOR THOUGHT

Pay attention to your hunger cues. Do you eat only when you're hungry? Do you stop eating when you're full? Or do you continue eating past the point of satiety? Do you eat because you see food and then decide you're hungry, or do you do an internal "gut check" before eating?

If you eat in response to cues in your environment and not because your body is telling you it needs to be nourished, think of ways you can change your eating environment for the better. How can you eliminate the external stimuli that have you eating even when you don't feel hungry?

STAGE 5 *Workout Log*

DATE | **COURSE:**

WORKOUT TIME/TYPE:

NOTES (include how you felt, weather, etc.): | **ADDITIONAL ACTIVITY:**

DATE | **COURSE:**

WORKOUT TIME/TYPE:

NOTES (include how you felt, weather, etc.): | **ADDITIONAL ACTIVITY:**

DATE | **COURSE:**

WORKOUT TIME/TYPE:

NOTES (include how you felt, weather, etc.): | **ADDITIONAL ACTIVITY:**

DATE | **COURSE:**

WORKOUT TIME/TYPE:

NOTES (include how you felt, weather, etc.): | **ADDITIONAL ACTIVITY:**

DATE | **COURSE:**

WORKOUT TIME/TYPE:

NOTES (include how you felt, weather, etc.): | **ADDITIONAL ACTIVITY:**

DATE		COURSE:	

WORKOUT TIME/TYPE:

NOTES (include how you felt, weather, etc.):	ADDITIONAL ACTIVITY:

DATE		COURSE:	

WORKOUT TIME/TYPE:

NOTES (include how you felt, weather, etc.):	ADDITIONAL ACTIVITY:

TOTAL WORKOUTS FOR THE WEEK:	TOTAL WALKING MINUTES FOR THE WEEK:

FOOD FOR THOUGHT

Leave your measuring cups and spoons on the kitchen counter so you'll see them and use them. For a few days, take the time to measure the foods you eat that don't come in single-serving sizes. Pay special attention to cereal, pasta, rice, and other grains as well as salad dressings, juice, and ice cream. Read the labels on food packaging so you can tell what a true serving size is and where you're exceeding it. If necessary, swap your plates and glasses for smaller ones so true servings fill up the vessels you're eating from. Take a few minutes to jot down what you learn from this process.

STAGE 6 *Workout Log*

DATE COURSE:

WORKOUT TIME/TYPE:

NOTES (include how you felt, weather, etc.): ADDITIONAL ACTIVITY:

DATE COURSE:

WORKOUT TIME/TYPE:

NOTES (include how you felt, weather, etc.): ADDITIONAL ACTIVITY:

DATE COURSE:

WORKOUT TIME/TYPE:

NOTES (include how you felt, weather, etc.): ADDITIONAL ACTIVITY:

DATE COURSE:

WORKOUT TIME/TYPE:

NOTES (include how you felt, weather, etc.): ADDITIONAL ACTIVITY:

DATE COURSE:

WORKOUT TIME/TYPE:

NOTES (include how you felt, weather, etc.): ADDITIONAL ACTIVITY:

DATE	COURSE:	
WORKOUT TIME/TYPE:		
NOTES (include how you felt, weather, etc.):		ADDITIONAL ACTIVITY:

DATE	COURSE:	
WORKOUT TIME/TYPE:		
NOTES (include how you felt, weather, etc.):		ADDITIONAL ACTIVITY:

TOTAL WORKOUTS FOR THE WEEK:	TOTAL WALKING MINUTES FOR THE WEEK:

FOOD LOG #2

On the following pages, record your second food log. As you did the first time you logged, keep track for 3 days, and try to include a weekend day. We're asking you to pay attention to two additional questions this time, so you'll notice this second food log is slightly different than the first one you kept. This time, also focus on the *amount* of food you ate (i.e., a 4-ounce steak or 1 cup of broccoli) as well as whether you were feeling hungry before your meal or snack.

WALK YOUR BUTT OFF! *Food Log*

TIME:	WHAT YOU ATE AND THE AMOUNT:	WHAT YOU DRANK:	WHERE WERE YOU?	WERE YOU HUNGRY? (Y/N)

WALK YOUR BUTT OFF! *Food Log*

TIME:	WHAT YOU ATE AND THE AMOUNT:	WHAT YOU DRANK:	WHERE WERE YOU?	WERE YOU HUNGRY? (Y/N)

WALK YOUR BUTT OFF! *Food Log*

TIME:	WHAT YOU ATE AND THE AMOUNT:	WHAT YOU DRANK:	WHERE WERE YOU?	WERE YOU HUNGRY? (Y/N)

FOOD FOR THOUGHT

Look at the log you just completed. Read it. This is a good time to do a calorie tally to get a sense of what you're consuming in a day. It's not something you need to think about *too* much if the idea of putting numbers on your food drives you nuts. All the same, it's good to have a ballpark idea of how many calories you're eating. Simple smartphone apps, like MyPlate and MyFood-a-Pedia, and sites like CalorieKing.com can give you a good idea.

Based on a recent food log, my average total daily calories: _____

Assess your eating progress. How are you doing on the biggest eating challenge you identified at the beginning of the workbook? If you've improved that point of concern, are you ready to try improving a different eating problem? Are there any meals or times during the day that are higher calorically than you expected? Jot down any observations you've made based on your most recent log.

WEIGHT THIS WEEK

STAGE 7 *Workout Log*

DATE		COURSE:

WORKOUT TIME/TYPE:

NOTES (include how you felt, weather, etc.): | ADDITIONAL ACTIVITY:

DATE		COURSE:

WORKOUT TIME/TYPE:

NOTES (include how you felt, weather, etc.): | ADDITIONAL ACTIVITY:

DATE		COURSE:

WORKOUT TIME/TYPE:

NOTES (include how you felt, weather, etc.): | ADDITIONAL ACTIVITY:

DATE		COURSE:

WORKOUT TIME/TYPE:

NOTES (include how you felt, weather, etc.): | ADDITIONAL ACTIVITY:

DATE		COURSE:

WORKOUT TIME/TYPE:

NOTES (include how you felt, weather, etc.): | ADDITIONAL ACTIVITY:

DATE		COURSE:
WORKOUT TIME/TYPE:		
NOTES (include how you felt, weather, etc.):		ADDITIONAL ACTIVITY:

DATE		COURSE:
WORKOUT TIME/TYPE:		
NOTES (include how you felt, weather, etc.):		ADDITIONAL ACTIVITY:
TOTAL WORKOUTS FOR THE WEEK:		TOTAL WALKING MINUTES FOR THE WEEK:

FOOD FOR THOUGHT

Getting enough protein in your diet is essential to fueling your body for exercise and keeping you full and satisfied longer after meals.

To figure out how much protein you need in a day, take your ideal body weight and divide it by 2. That's the number of grams of protein you need. For example, if your ideal weight is 150 pounds, you need 75 grams of protein in a day.

The number is likely higher than you realized. In order to eat enough, you'll have to find significant sources of protein to add to each meal of the day, not just dinner. Adding protein to breakfast and lunch will help control your appetite throughout the day.

My daily protein needs: _____ grams

WEIGHT THIS WEEK

STAGE 8 *Workout Log*

DATE	COURSE:

WORKOUT TIME/TYPE:

NOTES (include how you felt, weather, etc.):	ADDITIONAL ACTIVITY:

DATE	COURSE:

WORKOUT TIME/TYPE:

NOTES (include how you felt, weather, etc.):	ADDITIONAL ACTIVITY:

DATE	COURSE:

WORKOUT TIME/TYPE:

NOTES (include how you felt, weather, etc.):	ADDITIONAL ACTIVITY:

DATE	COURSE:

WORKOUT TIME/TYPE:

NOTES (include how you felt, weather, etc.):	ADDITIONAL ACTIVITY:

DATE	COURSE:

WORKOUT TIME/TYPE:

NOTES (include how you felt, weather, etc.):	ADDITIONAL ACTIVITY:

DATE	COURSE:
WORKOUT TIME/TYPE:	

NOTES (include how you felt, weather, etc.):	ADDITIONAL ACTIVITY:

DATE	COURSE:
WORKOUT TIME/TYPE:	

NOTES (include how you felt, weather, etc.):	ADDITIONAL ACTIVITY:

TOTAL WORKOUTS FOR THE WEEK:	TOTAL WALKING MINUTES FOR THE WEEK:

FOOD FOR THOUGHT

Think about how you define *snack*. A snack should be premeditated. A snack is an eating occasion, served from a plate, when you pay attention to the food going into your mouth and actually taste it. (It's not license to put your hand in a bag of pretzels and stuff a bunch in your mouth every few minutes.) If you're hungry for a snack, go ahead, but make sure it mimics a meal. Aim for 200 to 250 calories; include protein, fiber, carbohydrate, and a little fat; serve it from a plate; and have two items: an apple and a piece of cheese, for instance, or a mini pita with carrots and hummus. Based on those guidelines, brainstorm some snacks you'll make for yourself in the coming week.

WEIGHT THIS WEEK

STAGE 9 *Workout Log*

DATE COURSE:

WORKOUT TIME/TYPE:

NOTES (include how you felt, weather, etc.): ADDITIONAL ACTIVITY:

DATE COURSE:

WORKOUT TIME/TYPE:

NOTES (include how you felt, weather, etc.): ADDITIONAL ACTIVITY:

DATE COURSE:

WORKOUT TIME/TYPE:

NOTES (include how you felt, weather, etc.): ADDITIONAL ACTIVITY:

DATE COURSE:

WORKOUT TIME/TYPE:

NOTES (include how you felt, weather, etc.): ADDITIONAL ACTIVITY:

DATE COURSE:

WORKOUT TIME/TYPE:

NOTES (include how you felt, weather, etc.): ADDITIONAL ACTIVITY:

DATE		COURSE:

WORKOUT TIME/TYPE:

NOTES (include how you felt, weather, etc.):	ADDITIONAL ACTIVITY:

DATE		COURSE:

WORKOUT TIME/TYPE:

NOTES (include how you felt, weather, etc.):	ADDITIONAL ACTIVITY:

TOTAL WORKOUTS FOR THE WEEK:	TOTAL WALKING MINUTES FOR THE WEEK:

FOOD FOR THOUGHT

Go back to your most recent food log and tally your fiber intake. Women and men younger than age 50 need 25 to 38 grams of fiber per day. People older than age 50 need 21 to 30 grams a day. Most people don't get enough, and if you don't, look for swaps you can make at each meal to increase your fiber intake. The increase should be gradual, however; and be sure to drink plenty of water when you increase your fiber, to keep your digestive system functioning properly.

Adding colorful foods to each meal boosts your fiber consumption and nourishes your body with vitamins and minerals. Consider how you can add a fruit or vegetable—or both—to every meal and snack.

Breakfast: _____

Lunch: _____

Dinner: _____

Snacks: _____

STAGE 10 *Workout Log*

DATE	COURSE:

WORKOUT TIME/TYPE:

NOTES (include how you felt, weather, etc.): | ADDITIONAL ACTIVITY:

DATE	COURSE:

WORKOUT TIME/TYPE:

NOTES (include how you felt, weather, etc.): | ADDITIONAL ACTIVITY:

DATE	COURSE:

WORKOUT TIME/TYPE:

NOTES (include how you felt, weather, etc.): | ADDITIONAL ACTIVITY:

DATE	COURSE:

WORKOUT TIME/TYPE:

NOTES (include how you felt, weather, etc.): | ADDITIONAL ACTIVITY:

DATE	COURSE:

WORKOUT TIME/TYPE:

NOTES (include how you felt, weather, etc.): | ADDITIONAL ACTIVITY:

DATE	COURSE:

WORKOUT TIME/TYPE:

NOTES (include how you felt, weather, etc.):	ADDITIONAL ACTIVITY:

DATE	COURSE:

WORKOUT TIME/TYPE:

NOTES (include how you felt, weather, etc.):	ADDITIONAL ACTIVITY:

TOTAL WORKOUTS FOR THE WEEK:	TOTAL WALKING MINUTES FOR THE WEEK:

FOOD LOG #3

This is your final food log. As you have done previously, keep track for at least 3 days and try to include a weekend day. This final log includes two new columns for protein (P) and fiber (F). Use the prompts from Stages 7 and 9 to define your protein and fiber goals. You can find this info listed on the nutrition label of packaged food and on Web sites like CalorieKing.com.

WALK YOUR BUTT OFF! *Food Log*

TIME:	WHAT YOU ATE AND THE AMOUNT:	WHAT YOU DRANK:	WHERE WERE YOU?	WERE YOU HUNGRY? Y/N	P (G)	F (G)

WALK YOUR BUTT OFF! *Food Log*

TIME:	WHAT YOU ATE AND THE AMOUNT:	WHAT YOU DRANK:	WHERE WERE YOU?	WERE YOU HUNGRY? Y/N	P (G)	F (G)

WALK YOUR BUTT OFF! *Food Log*

TIME:	WHAT YOU ATE AND THE AMOUNT:	WHAT YOU DRANK:	WHERE WERE YOU?	WERE YOU HUNGRY? Y/N	P (G)	F (G)

WALK YOUR BUTT OFF! *Food Log*

TIME:	WHAT YOU ATE AND THE AMOUNT:	WHAT YOU DRANK:	WHERE WERE YOU?	WERE YOU HUNGRY? Y/N	P (G)	F (G)

STAGE 11 *Workout Log*

DATE	COURSE:

WORKOUT TIME/TYPE:

NOTES (include how you felt, weather, etc.): | **ADDITIONAL ACTIVITY:**

DATE	COURSE:

WORKOUT TIME/TYPE:

NOTES (include how you felt, weather, etc.): | **ADDITIONAL ACTIVITY:**

DATE	COURSE:

WORKOUT TIME/TYPE:

NOTES (include how you felt, weather, etc.): | **ADDITIONAL ACTIVITY:**

DATE	COURSE:

WORKOUT TIME/TYPE:

NOTES (include how you felt, weather, etc.): | **ADDITIONAL ACTIVITY:**

DATE	COURSE:

WORKOUT TIME/TYPE:

NOTES (include how you felt, weather, etc.): | **ADDITIONAL ACTIVITY:**

DATE	COURSE:

WORKOUT TIME/TYPE:

NOTES (include how you felt, weather, etc.):	ADDITIONAL ACTIVITY:

DATE	COURSE:

WORKOUT TIME/TYPE:

NOTES (include how you felt, weather, etc.):	ADDITIONAL ACTIVITY:

TOTAL WORKOUTS FOR THE WEEK:	TOTAL WALKING MINUTES FOR THE WEEK:

FOOD FOR THOUGHT

Look at your final log. When you compare it to the first log you kept, where have you been able to improve your eating? What times and meals are still problematic for you?

STAGE 12 *Workout Log*

DATE COURSE:

WORKOUT TIME/TYPE:

NOTES (include how you felt, weather, etc.): ADDITIONAL ACTIVITY:

DATE COURSE:

WORKOUT TIME/TYPE:

NOTES (include how you felt, weather, etc.): ADDITIONAL ACTIVITY:

DATE COURSE:

WORKOUT TIME/TYPE:

NOTES (include how you felt, weather, etc.): ADDITIONAL ACTIVITY:

DATE COURSE:

WORKOUT TIME/TYPE:

NOTES (include how you felt, weather, etc.): ADDITIONAL ACTIVITY:

DATE COURSE:

WORKOUT TIME/TYPE:

NOTES (include how you felt, weather, etc.): ADDITIONAL ACTIVITY:

DATE	COURSE:
WORKOUT TIME/TYPE:	

NOTES (include how you felt, weather, etc.):	ADDITIONAL ACTIVITY:

DATE	COURSE:
WORKOUT TIME/TYPE:	

NOTES (include how you felt, weather, etc.):	ADDITIONAL ACTIVITY:

TOTAL WORKOUTS FOR THE WEEK:	TOTAL WALKING MINUTES FOR THE WEEK:

FOOD FOR THOUGHT

Do you find yourself overwhelmed by food cravings? Here's a strategy for dealing with them: First, identify what it is that you really want. Second, have some of that food. Be mindful of the quantity; a small amount of chocolate can go a long way. Third, acknowledge what you've done, tell yourself you feel better, and move on.

To help yourself going forward, think about your cravings, when they strike, and how you can satisfy them in a controlled way. Do you find yourself having cravings after a stressful work meeting or at night? Before you go about indulging every desire, ask yourself if you can modify your environment to reduce the cravings. Put food away that's sitting out or plan to take a walk instead of eating in response to stressful situations.

ACKNOWLEDGMENTS

A huge thank-you to Sarah, who writes the talk, and Michele, who walks the walk. It has been a privilege to work with both of you. And to all our test panelists who moved it, logged it, and ate it, thank you for getting off your butts and out the door and sharing your journeys with me.

—Leslie Bonci

Thanks to the fearless members of our test panel for your time, energy, and willingness to try this program. Without you—Steve Cobb, Deb Davies, Susan DeSmet, Val Donohue, Jennifer Durham, Crystal Dye, Gail Fragassi, Denise Getchell, Sandra Hamill, Judd Hark, Gayle Hendricks, Becca Kahle, Donna Karoly, William Kealey, Bethany Lee, Jacqueline Macaione, Margaret McConville, Charlene Nelson, Lori Powell, Arlene Scott, Kristen Tomasic, and Lorraine Weidorn—this project would not have been possible. In making your triumphs and struggles an open book, you've made a better book for everyone.

Credit goes to my coauthors, Leslie and Michele, for your expertise and enthusiasm, and to our editor, Marielle Messing, for your thoughtful guidance throughout the process. Thank you, Janet Fu McDevitt, for sharing your cooking acumen during our recipe development process. Kudos to Caitlyn Diimig, a big help with research. And thanks especially to my family, Charlie, Leah, and Ben, for all your support.

—Sarah Lorge Butler

To everyone I've ever walked with, thank you! You all inspire me and are the reasons I love what I do. A special thank-you to my husband, Andrew; son, Jacob; and daughter, Mia, for your love, support, and our after-dinner walks around our neighborhood.

—Michele Stanten

INDEX

Boldface page references indicate illustrations or photographs. <u>Underscored</u> references indicate boxed text.

Injury, 120
Insulation, for cold days, 140
Interval walks, 236–38, 238

J

Jacket, wind- and waterproof, 140
Juice
  serving size for, 108
  tart cherry, 196–97
Junk food, disposal of, 59–60

K

Kahle, Becca (test panelist), **172**, 172
Karoly, Donna (test panelist), **121**, 121
Kashi bar, 62
Kashi Cinnamon Harvest, 87
Kellogg's Special K, 195

L

Laddering workouts, 155–56
Landing
  softly, quietly, 170
  on your heels, 70, 72
Laughing Cow cheese wedges, 62
Laundry, folding, 155
Leaning back, avoiding, 156, 156
Lee, Bethany (test panelist), **161**, 161
Leg lift, table top, 80–81, **80–81**
Leg strength, 75
Legumes
  as fiber source, 194
  health benefits of, 197
Lettuce
  Fish Tacos, 180

Light on your feet, 170
Liquids
  with breakfast, 87
  daily amount needed, 158
  with lunch, 127
  reminders to drink, 157–58
  roles in body, 158
L.L.Bean, 141
Location
  for Challenge walk, 99–100
  for walking, 68–70
Log
  food log
    assessment for progress with eating challenges, 141–42
    assessment of average total daily calories, 265
    assessment of early entries in, 55
    benefits of, 36, 37, 37
    described, 34, 245
    example, 35, 38, 124, 218, 219, 245
    fiber tracking in, 195
    hunger tracking, 124
    portion size, recording, 124–25
    protein and fiber recorded in, 217, 273–77
    Stage 1, 247–51
    Stage 6, 124–25, 261–65
    Stage 10, 273–77
    Stage 11, 217, 220–21
    test panelists, 37–39, 38, 217–20
  Workout log
    described, 244
    example, 244
    Stage 1, 246–47
    Stage 2, 252–53
    Stage 3, 254–55
    Stage 4, 256–57
    Stage 5, 258–59
    Stage 6, 260–61

Stage 7, 266–67
Stage 8, 268–69
Stage 9, 270–71
Stage 10, 272–73
Stage 11, 278–79
Stage 12, 280–81
Long walks, 232
Loosening your hips, 210, 212
Luna bar, 62
Lunch
  amping up, 126–27
  fiber in, 196
  fruits and vegetables in, 198
  significance of, 125
  timing allotted to, 174
Lycopene, 197

M

Macaione, Jacqueline (test panelist), **159**, 159
Mandarin oranges
  Asian Salad, 179
  at dinner, 198
Mango, 198
Mapmyrun, 210
Mayo, serving size for, 108
McConville, Margaret (test panelist), 89
McDonald's, 194–95
McGovern, Dave (racewalker), 209
Meals
  breakfast
    calories in, 86
    characteristics of ideal, 86–87
    dessert with, 86
    fats in, 87
    fiber in, 195
    fluid intake at, 87
    fruits and vegetables in, 87, 198
    holiday survival guide, 128
    hunger suppression, 86, 90
    importance of, 86
    as meal, 87